BASCOVE

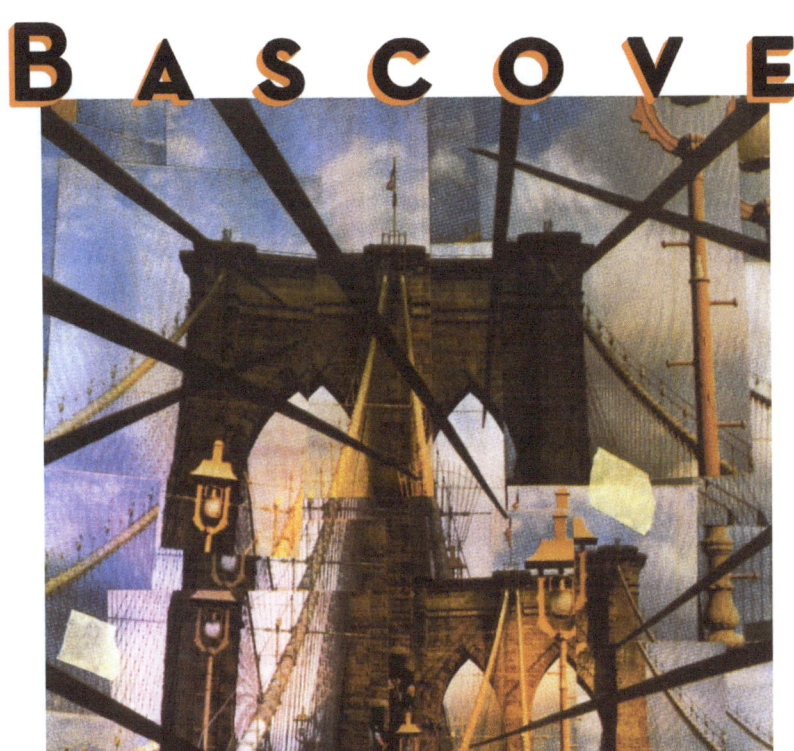

Title page

Brooklyn Bridge Erratica II detail

Bascove / Bridges
Transporting the Metropolis

Essays by Erin Urban
& John Baeder
Interview by Steven Jay Griffle

The Noble Maritime Collection
1000 Richmond Terrace, Staten Island, New York

As a museum on the waterfront, the Noble Maritime Collection is in touch with its transformations, and in 2010 we learned that the Bayonne Bridge had to be raised in order to accommodate the monster container ships that pass beneath it on the Kill van Kull. If it was not raised, the great Port of New York would lose its viability. The container ship traffic on the Kill, one of the busiest waterways in the world, would be routed to other ports on the Atlantic.

Nonetheless as artists and historians of the Port, we were dismayed that one of the great works of Othmar Ammann, who designed six of the most famous bridges in New York City, would be marred. Since the Bayonne was one of Ammann's favorite constructions—and it is the favorite bridge of most Staten Islanders—we decided that an homage was in order. Thus *Lifespan: The Bayonne Bridge in Transition*, an exhibition that looked at its history, contemporary artistic interpretations, and an explanation of the upcoming change in the mighty structure, came into being.

Thus our relationship with Bascove was born. As we searched for artists who painted, photographed, or drew the bridge, and got Noble's drawing of it's construction and his plans, photographs and records about it, we came upon an artist whose spirit is kindred to his. He lamented the fact that "about 20 ferry runs have died… since 1928, killed by a Port Authority bridge." She sees bridges as connections. He wrote that "each rotting ferry slip is a screaming memorial to a step toward making New York a duller and more inconvenient place to live. Each a mighty and decisive step toward our total enslavement by the automobile." She sees bridges as mighty and decisive spans that have "a sense of being suspended in a place that has an existence from either side." His exacting detail would have met its match in her exuberant forms. Their philosophies may have clashed, but oh the debates that would have ensued….

Erin Urban, Director, Noble Maritime Collection

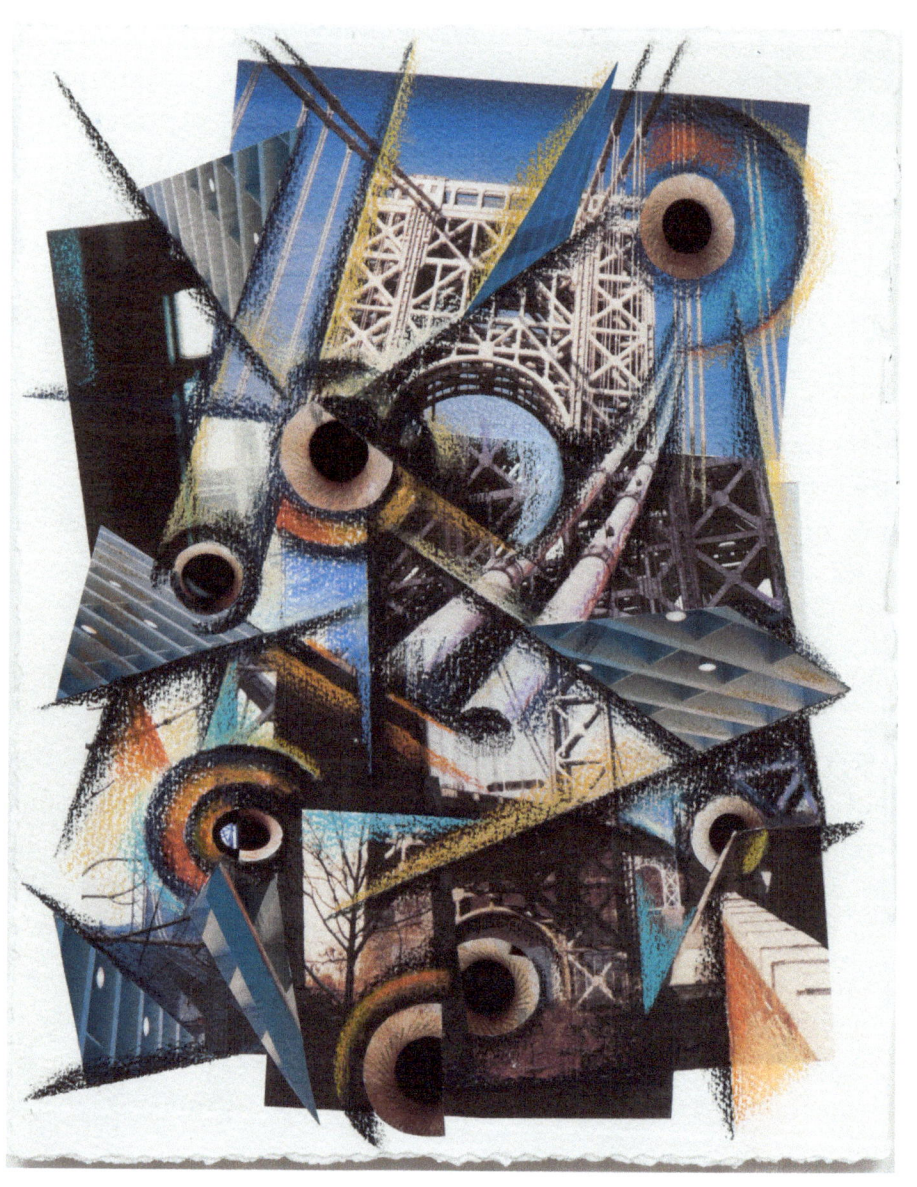

George Washington Bridge, 2011, pigment print, drawing & collage, 11" x 8 1/2"

WHEN I FIRST SAW BASCOVE

When I first saw Bascove's early drawings, gouaches, and prints, she was highly reticent in showing them. They were very personal, very deep, and very alive with vigor. I was still an agency art director and so overwhelmed, knowing immediately she needed proper exposure. Treasures were to be had.

Within a short matter of time, art directors were clamoring for her work. Her continual presence led her to a plethora of book cover illustrations. Bascove's strong spiritual and political ideologies allowed her to follow and do paintings and woodcuts for T. C. Boyle, J. M. Coetzee, and a host of other influential authors. The most notable series were the widely read (and much copied) book covers created for Robinson Davies. They rapidly became iconic. Bascove had the honor of being one of the top illustrators in the U.S.

She began to break the fine line from illustrator to full time painter, leaving her illustration career, and concentrating on gallery exhibits. Her prolific ideas led to other books accompanied by her beloved poets. Those specific paintings had overwhelming power and punch displaying inner strength, not just as a person, all her artistic capabilities. The most prominent is her New York Bridge series in STONE & STEEL. This book honors the architectural events we all take for granted. Appropriate poems accompany and highlight her dramatic images.

As with many painters, we all have to move on and explore new energies, Bascove has a warehouse full. Her recent collages are electrifying. Her ideas, a continuum of early work, are bold, fresh, and exhilarating. So exciting, they sparkle and stun the viewer.

They defy tradition and technique. Meticulous marvels, carefully thought out assembly of multiple elements that are magically focused into a giant explosion.

With a newfound energy, an energy akin to spontaneous combustion, supercharged sparkle that stuns the viewer. Breaks are needed to return for newfound moments that not only dazzle, but offer a variety of surprise after surprise.

Astonishingly, she continues her long held sense of commitment and dedication to her craft, with glowing ease and grace. Above all, Bascove's power of imagery has changed lives. She has mine.

JOHN BAEDER, 2014

BAYONNE BRIDGE I, 2003, oil on canvas, 42" x 26"

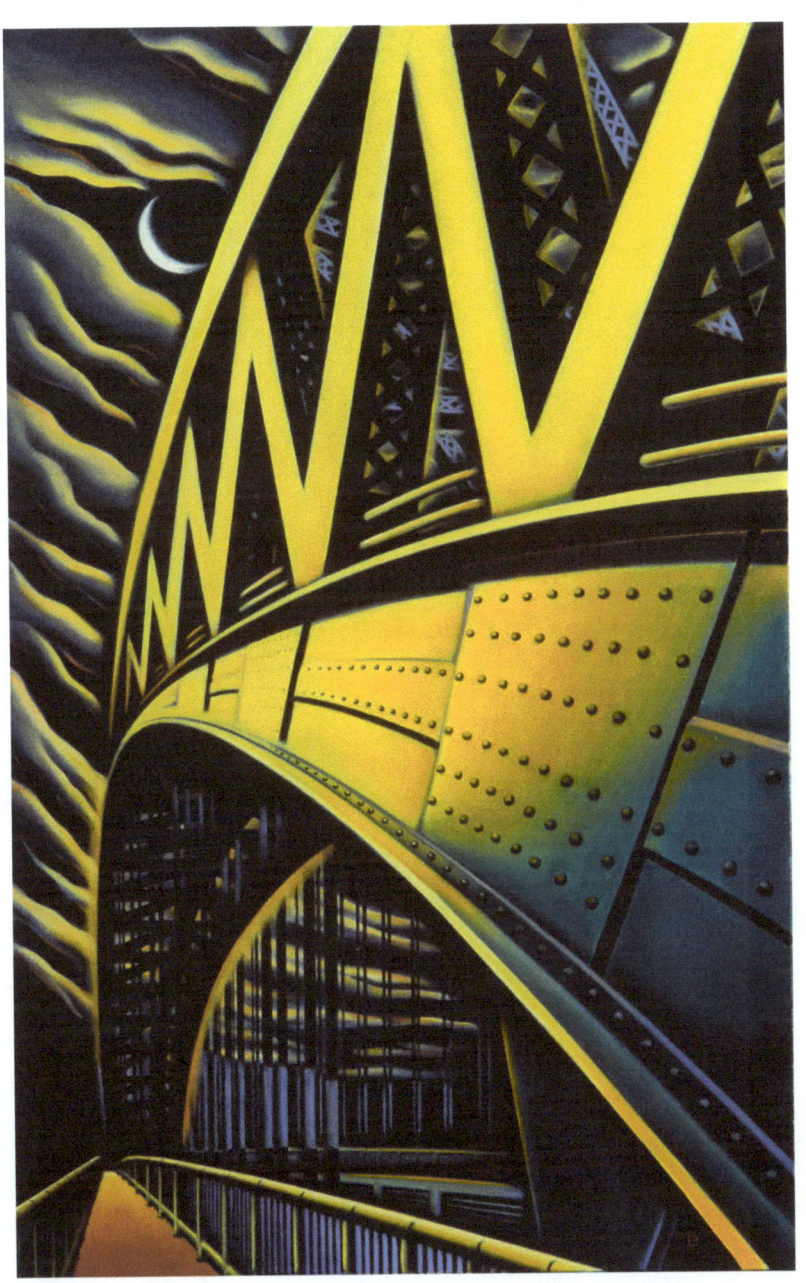

Bayonne Bridge II, 2003, oil on canvas, 26" x 52"

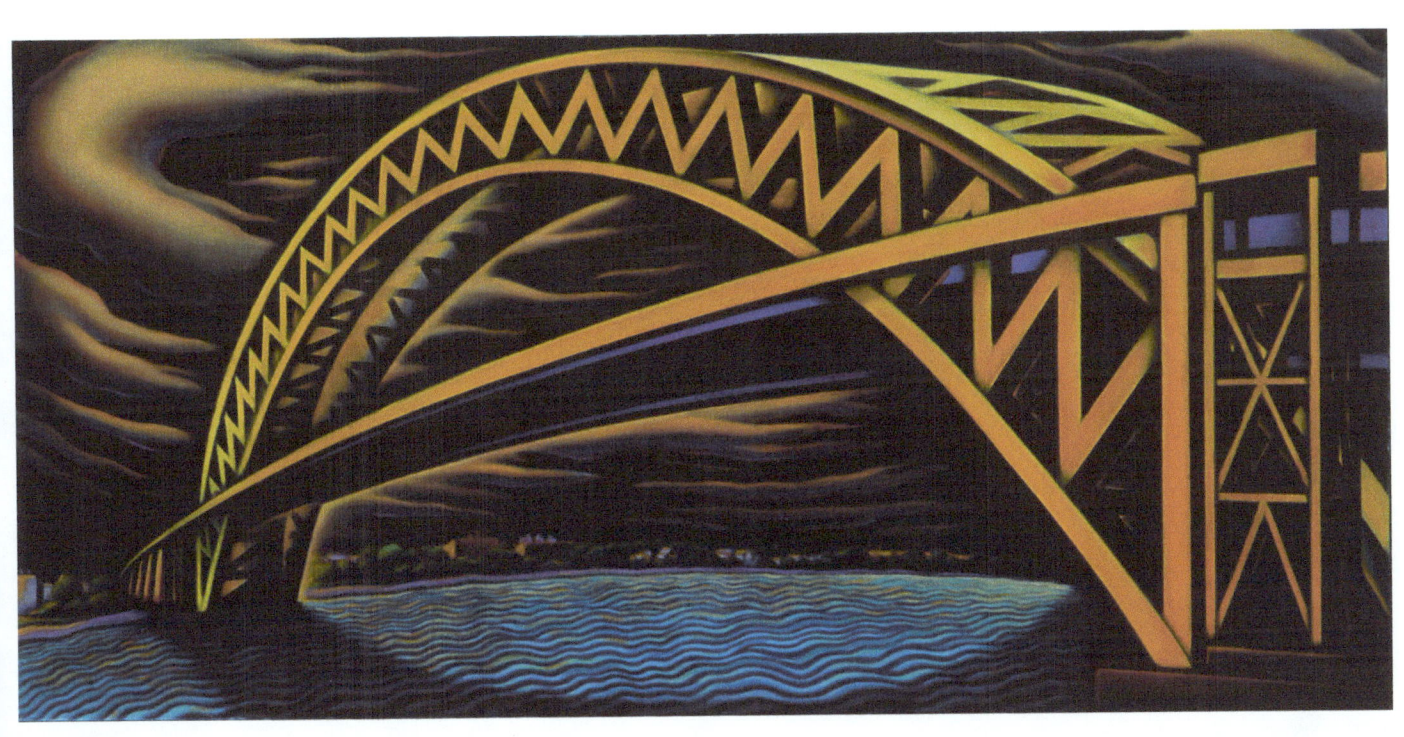

Harlem River Bridges III, 1998, oil on canvas, 30" x 48"

Collection of David and Natalya Bythewood

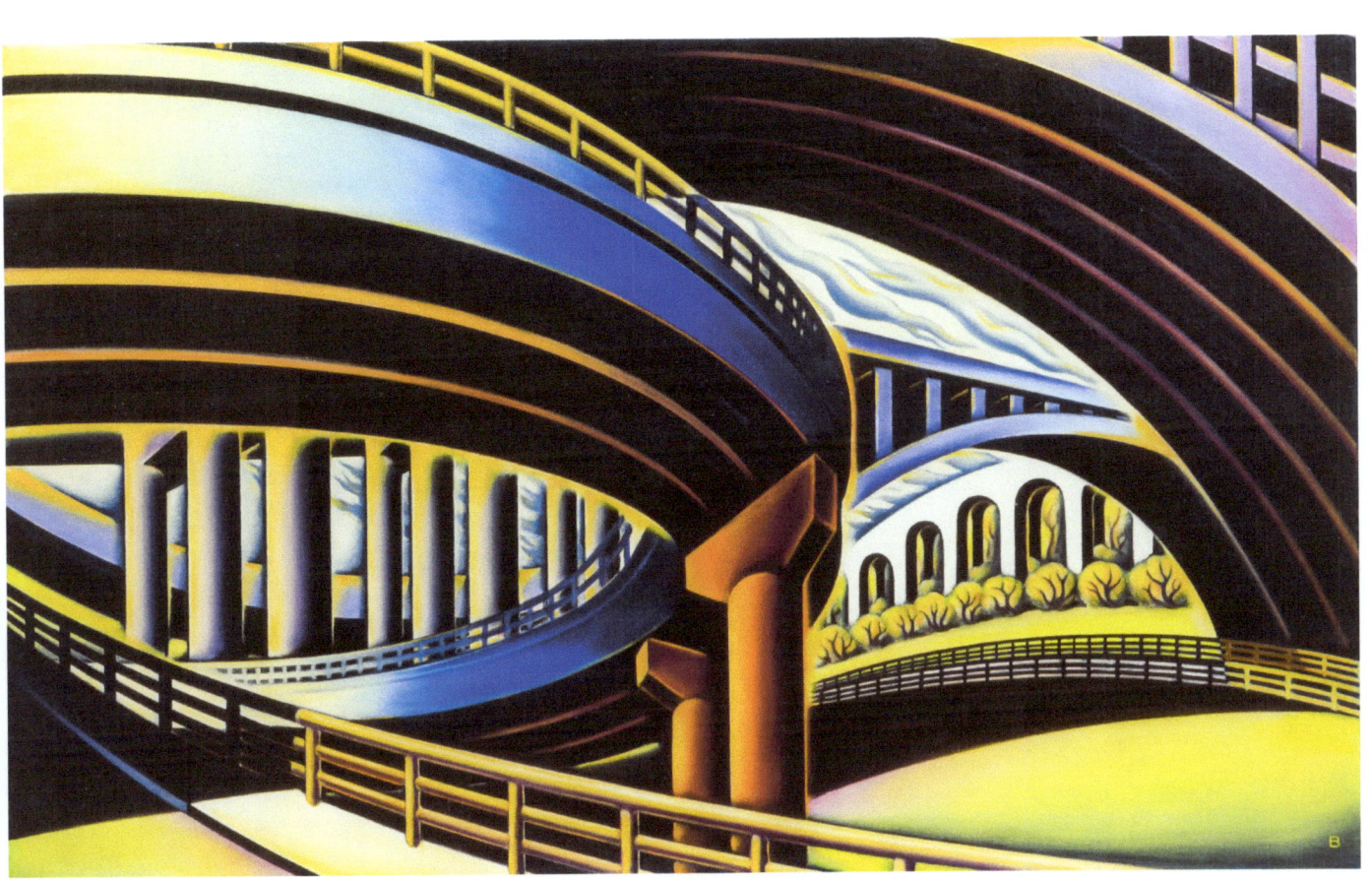

BRONX WHITESTONE BRIDGE, 1998, oil on canvas, 30" x 48"

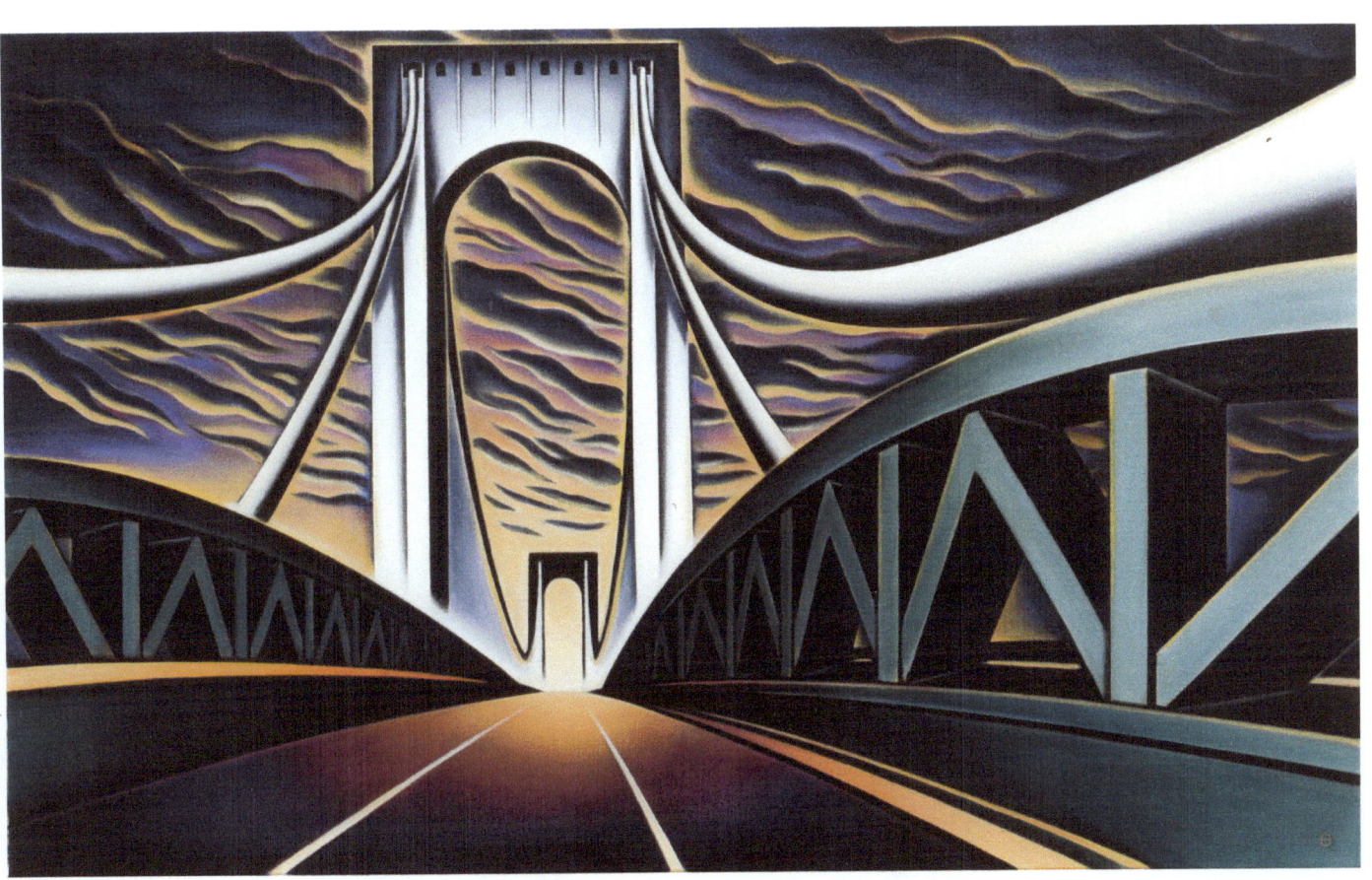

CASCIANO MEMORIAL BRIDGE, 2003, oil on canvas, 30" x 30"

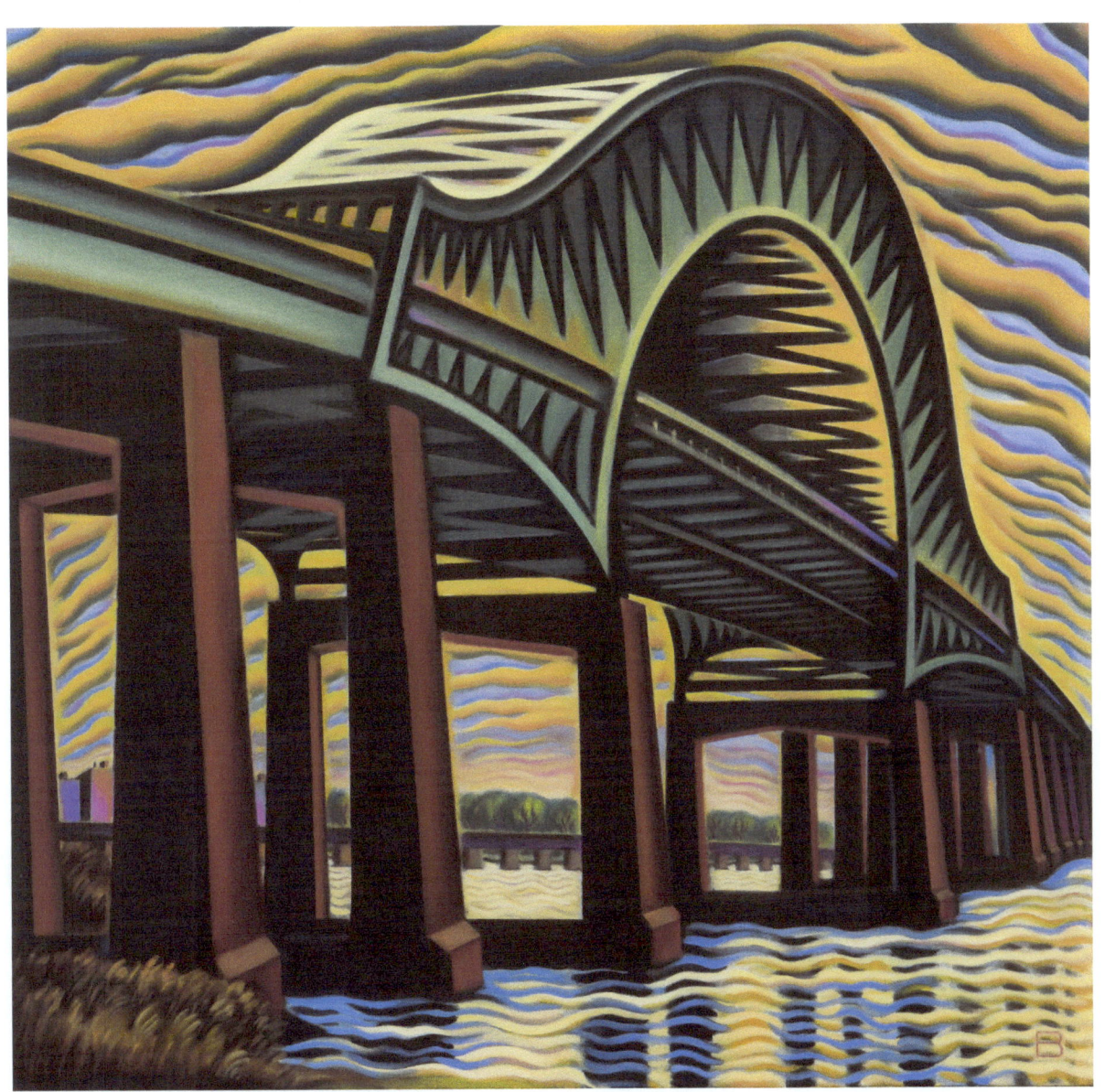

VERRAZANO-NARROWS BRIDGE, 1996, oil on canvas, 26" x 42"

Collection of Carol and Robert Linn

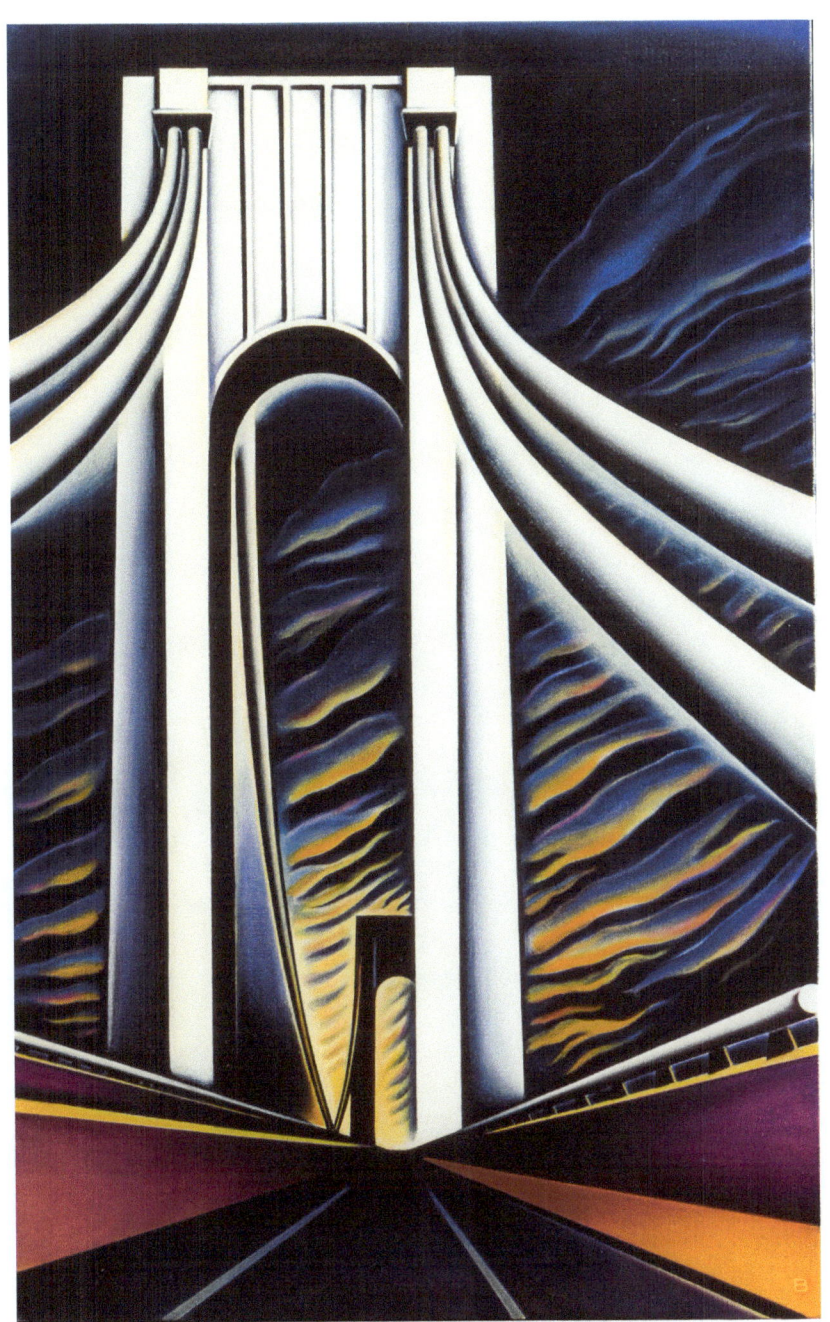

MANHATTAN BRIDGE, 1997, oil on canvas, 26" x 42"

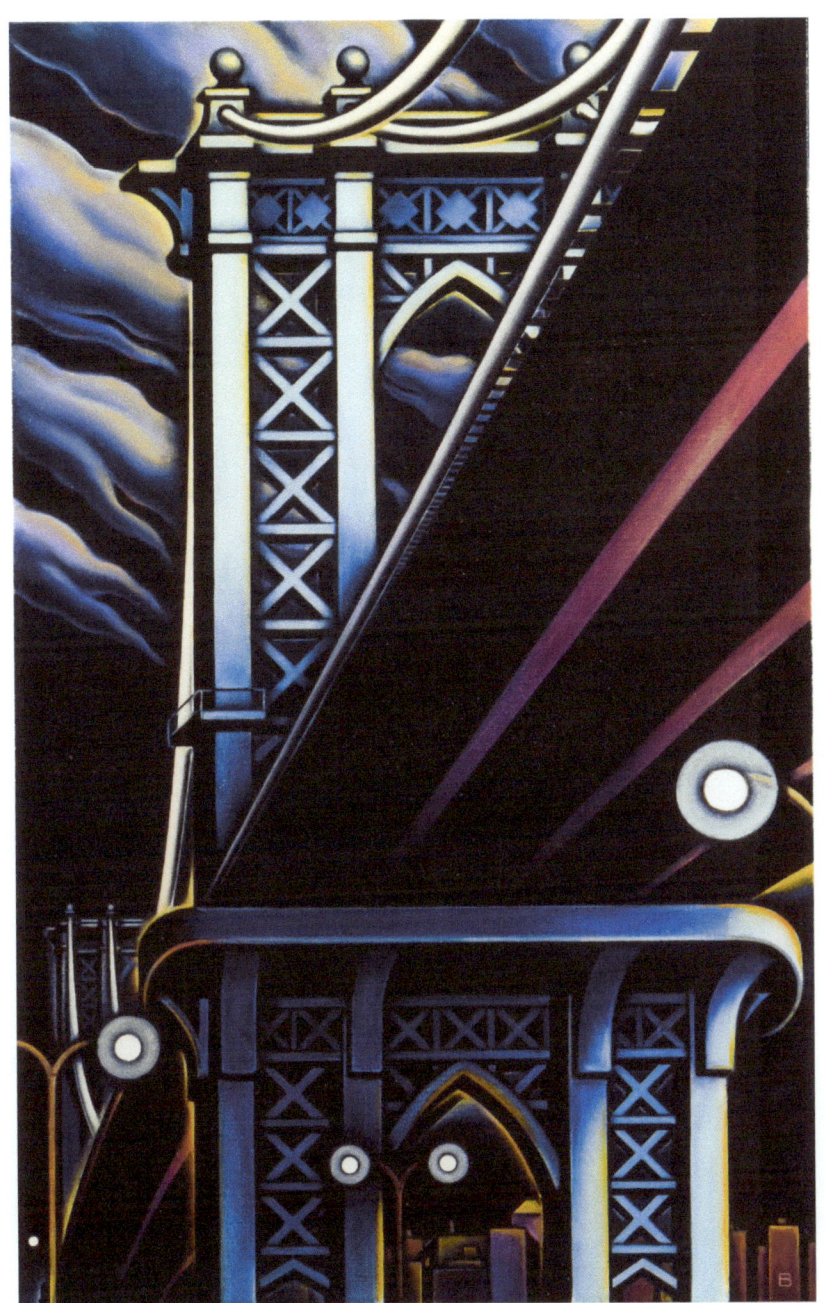

BROOKLYN BRIDGE III, 2001, oil on canvas, 30" x 30"

Collection of William and Scotti Tomson

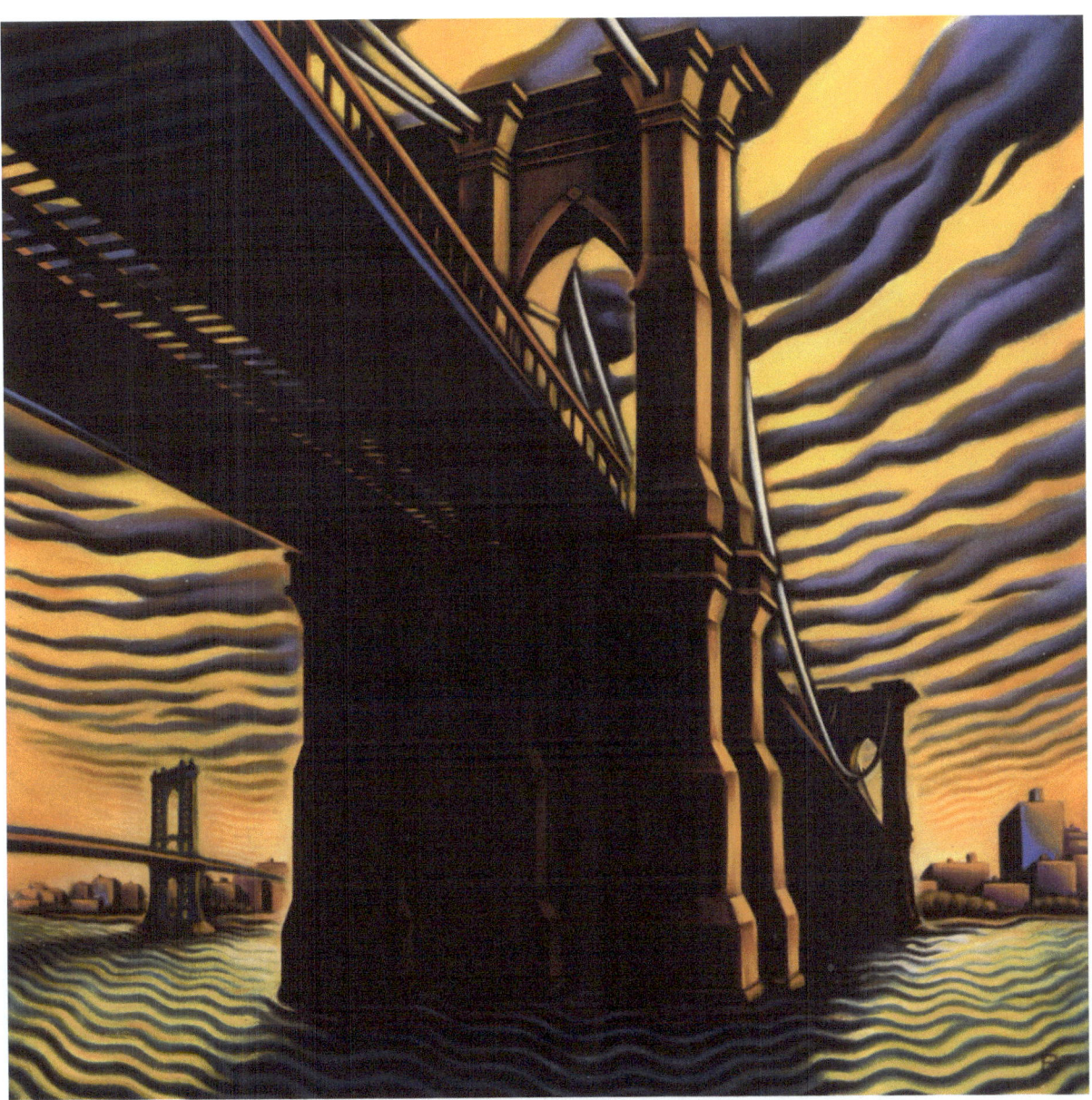

GEORGE WASHINGTON BRIDGE, 1997, oil on canvas, 30" x 30"

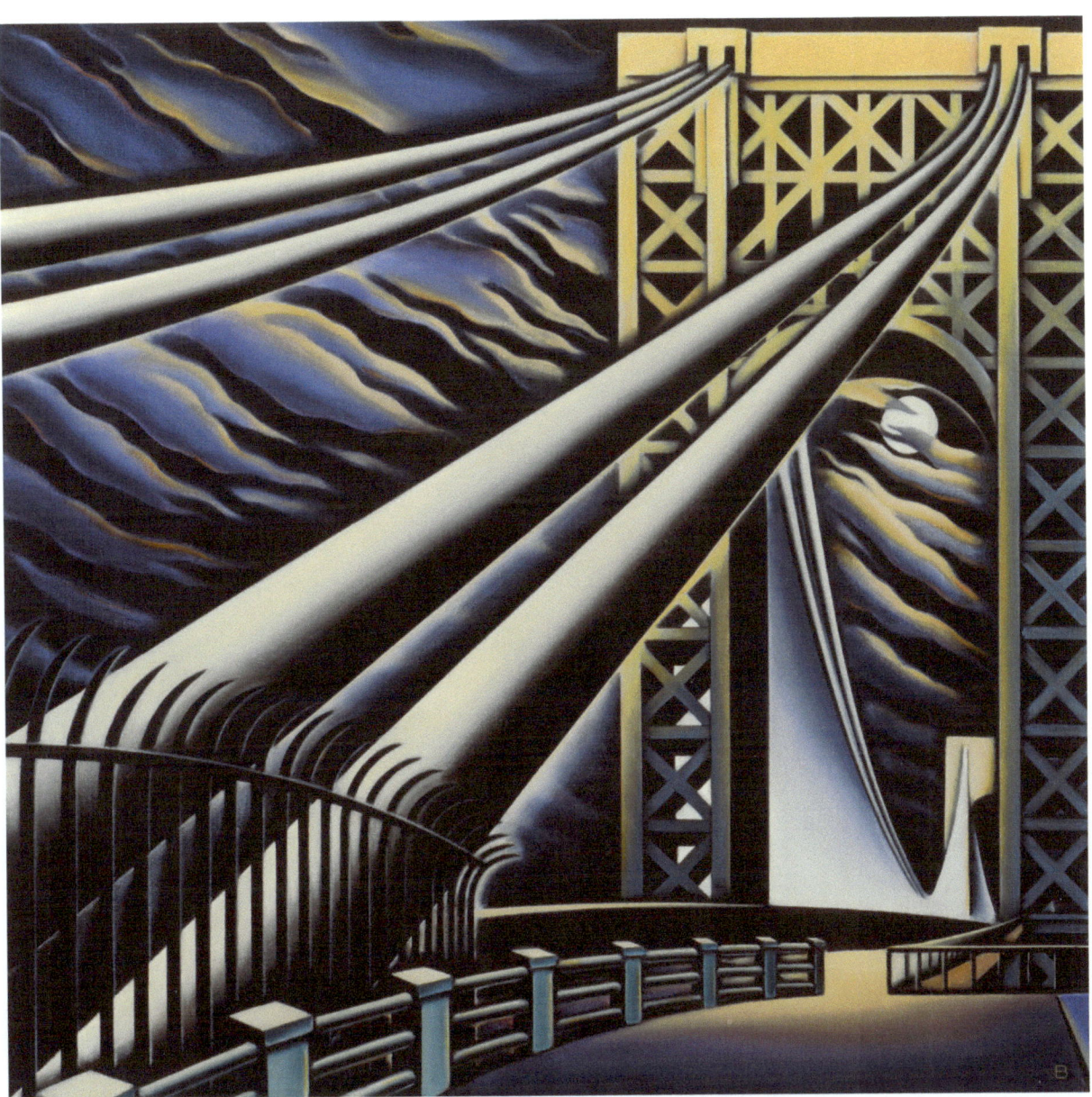

BROOKLYN BRIDGE IV, 2007, oil on canvas, 60" x 40"

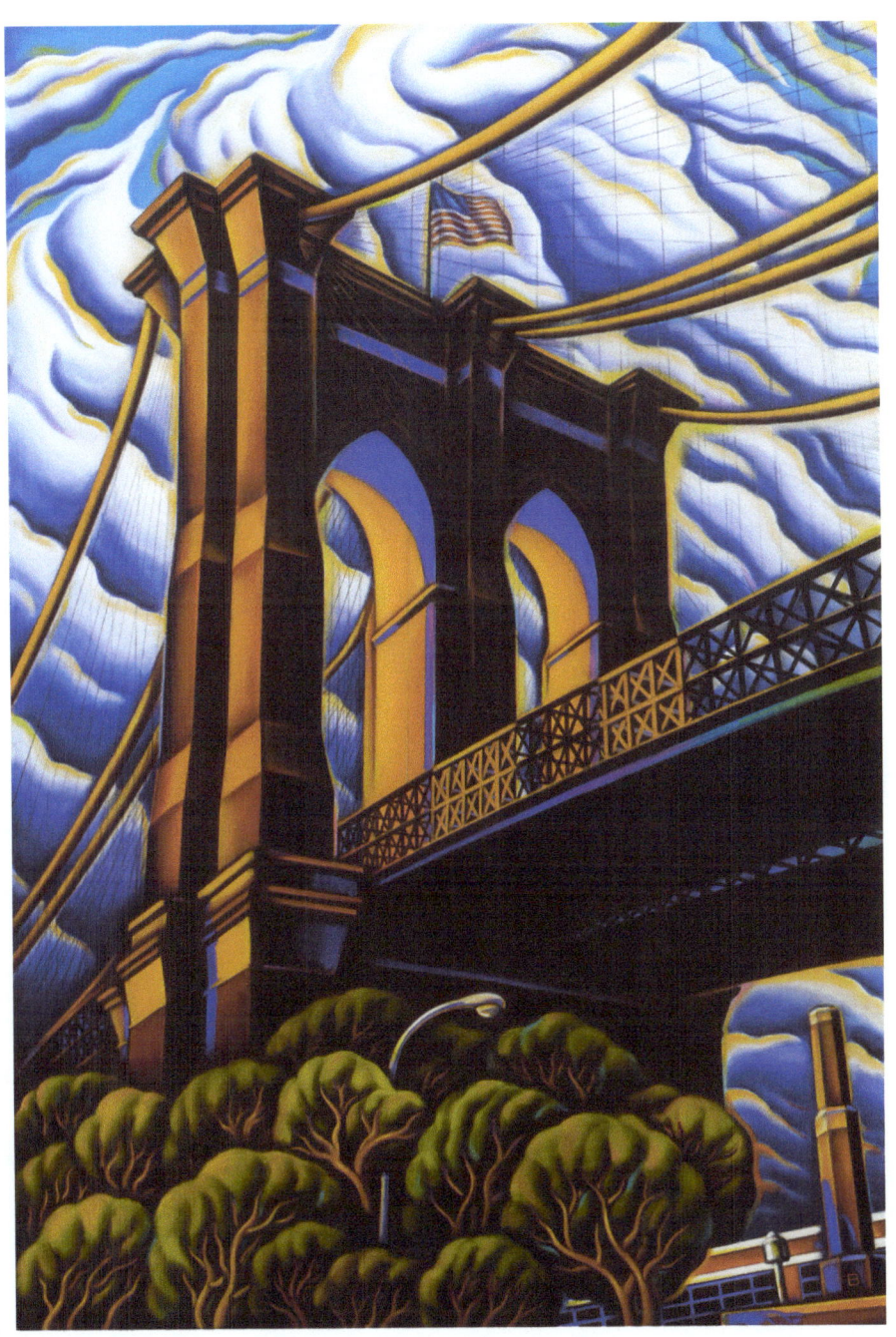

Queensborough Bridge III, 2005, oil on canvas, 30" x 60"

Collection of Carol and Robert Linn

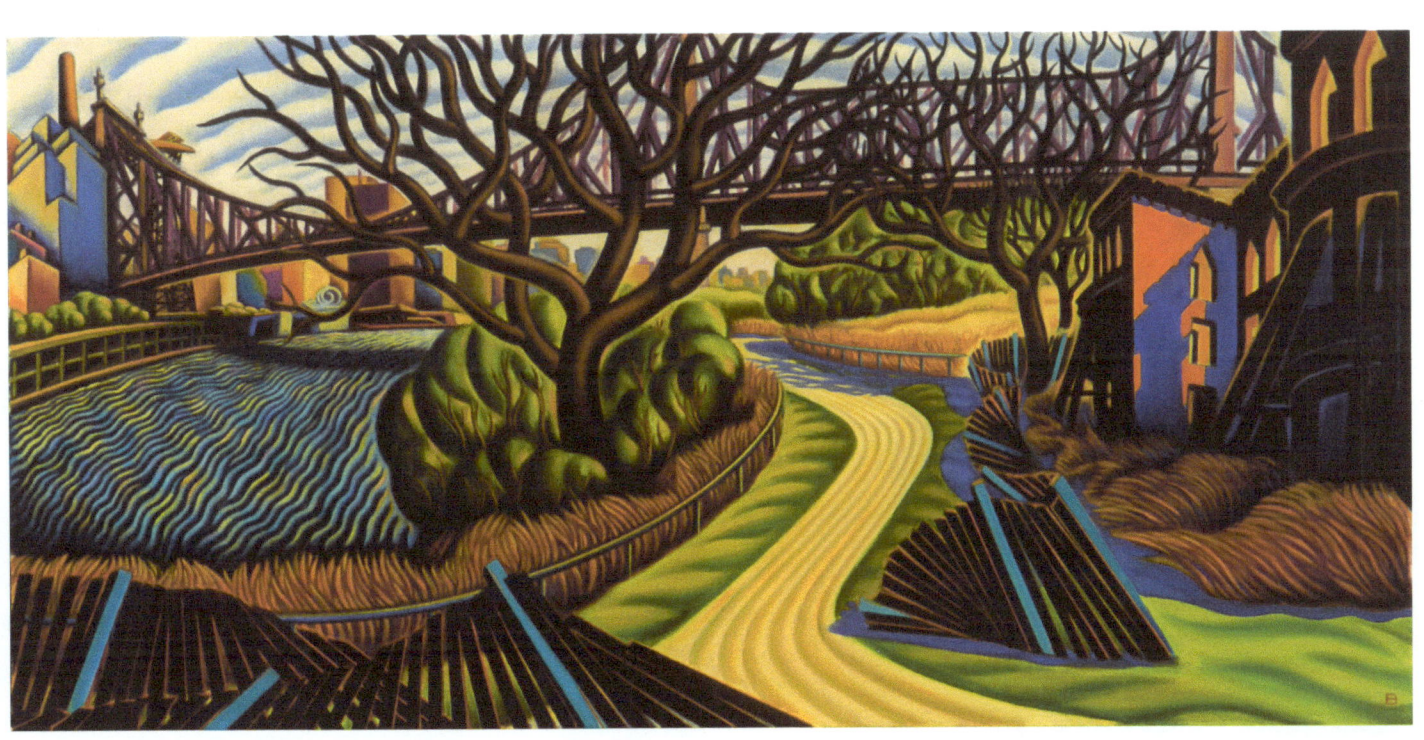

MACOMBS DAM BRIDGE, 2001, oil on canvas, 30" x 30"

Private Collection

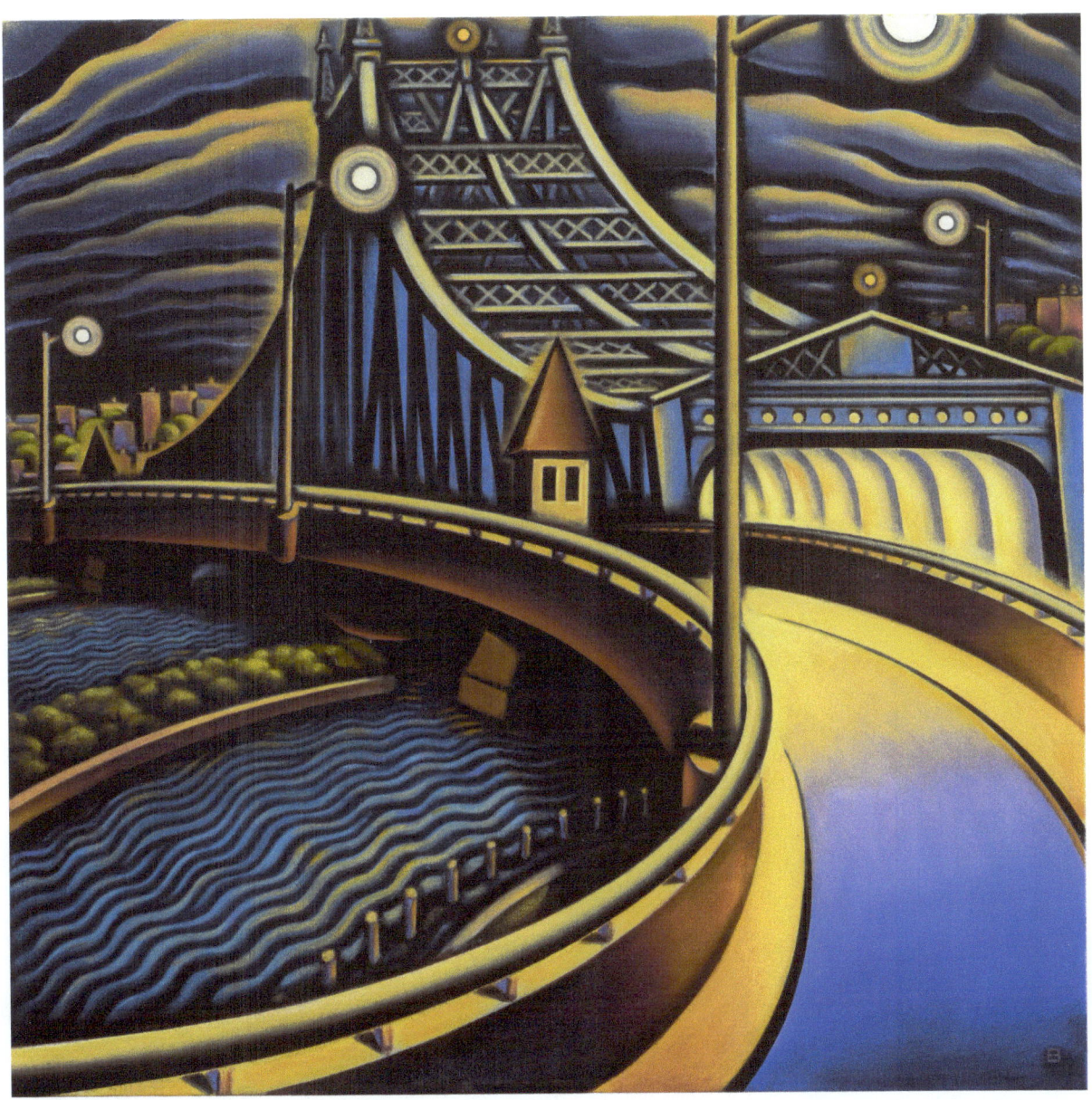

WILLIAMSBURG BRIDGE, 1995, oil on canvas, 30" x 30"

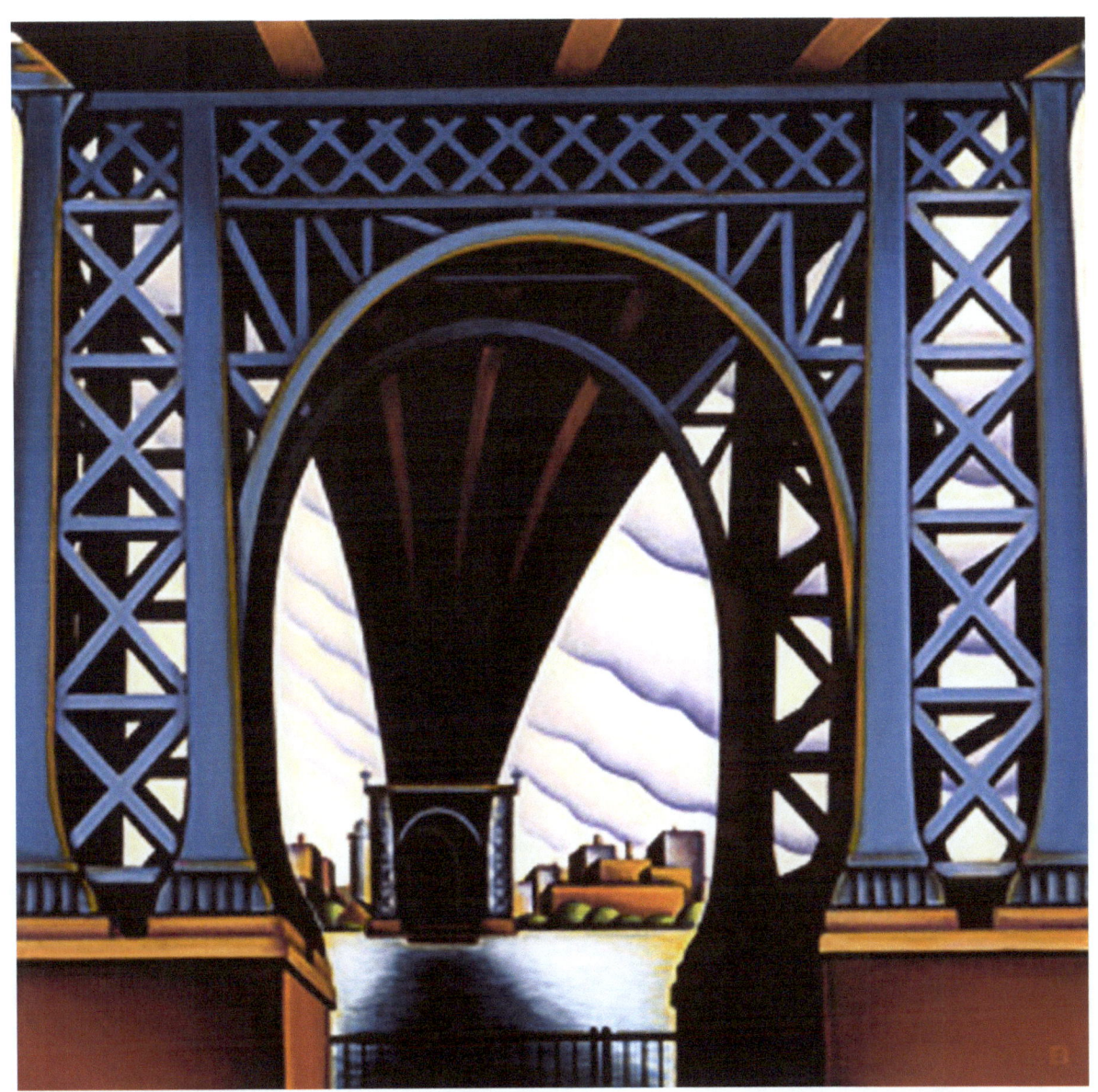

Brooklyn Bridge V, 2007, oil on canvas, 35" x 45"

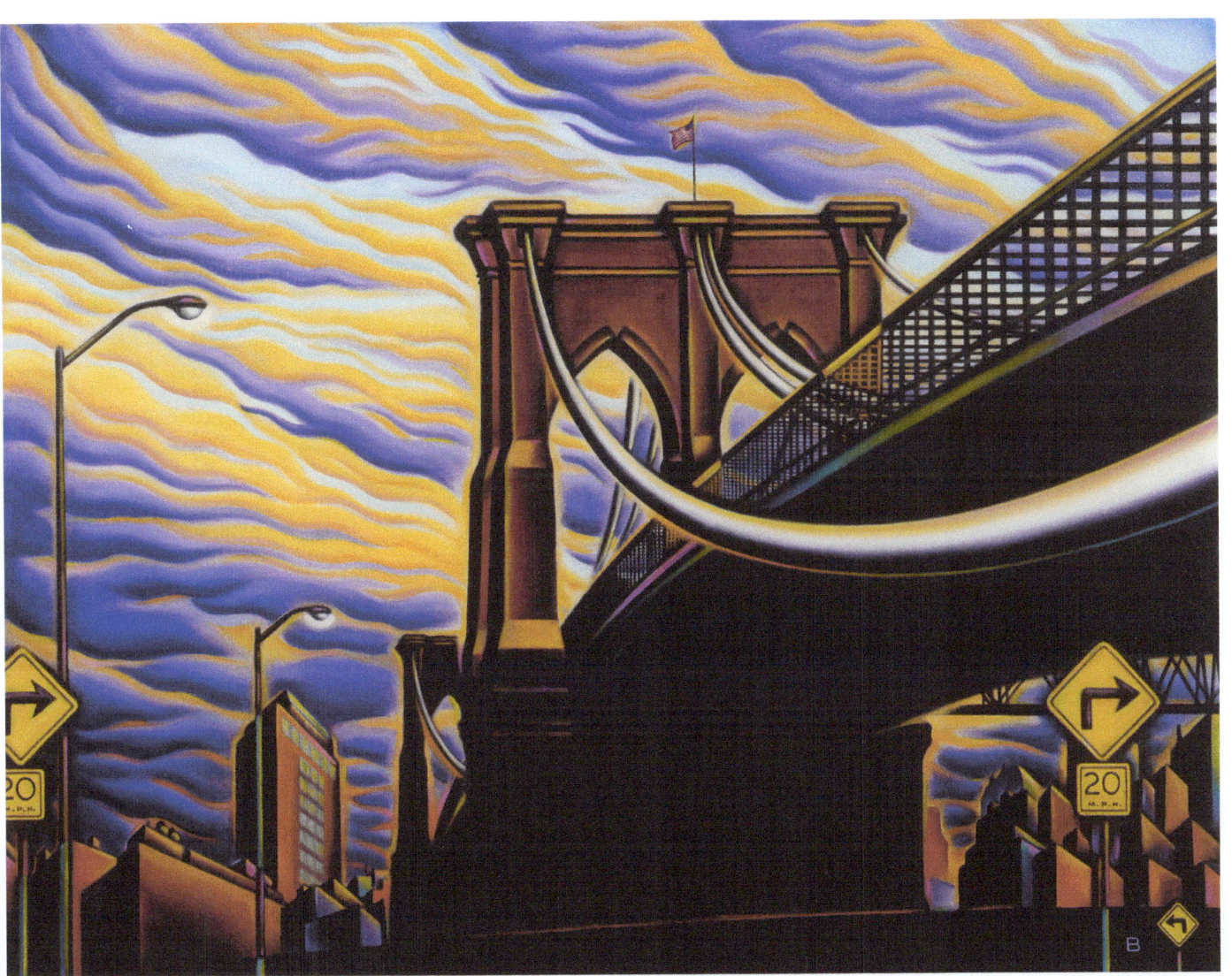

TRIBOROUGH BRIDGE II, 2000, oil on canvas, 30" x 48"

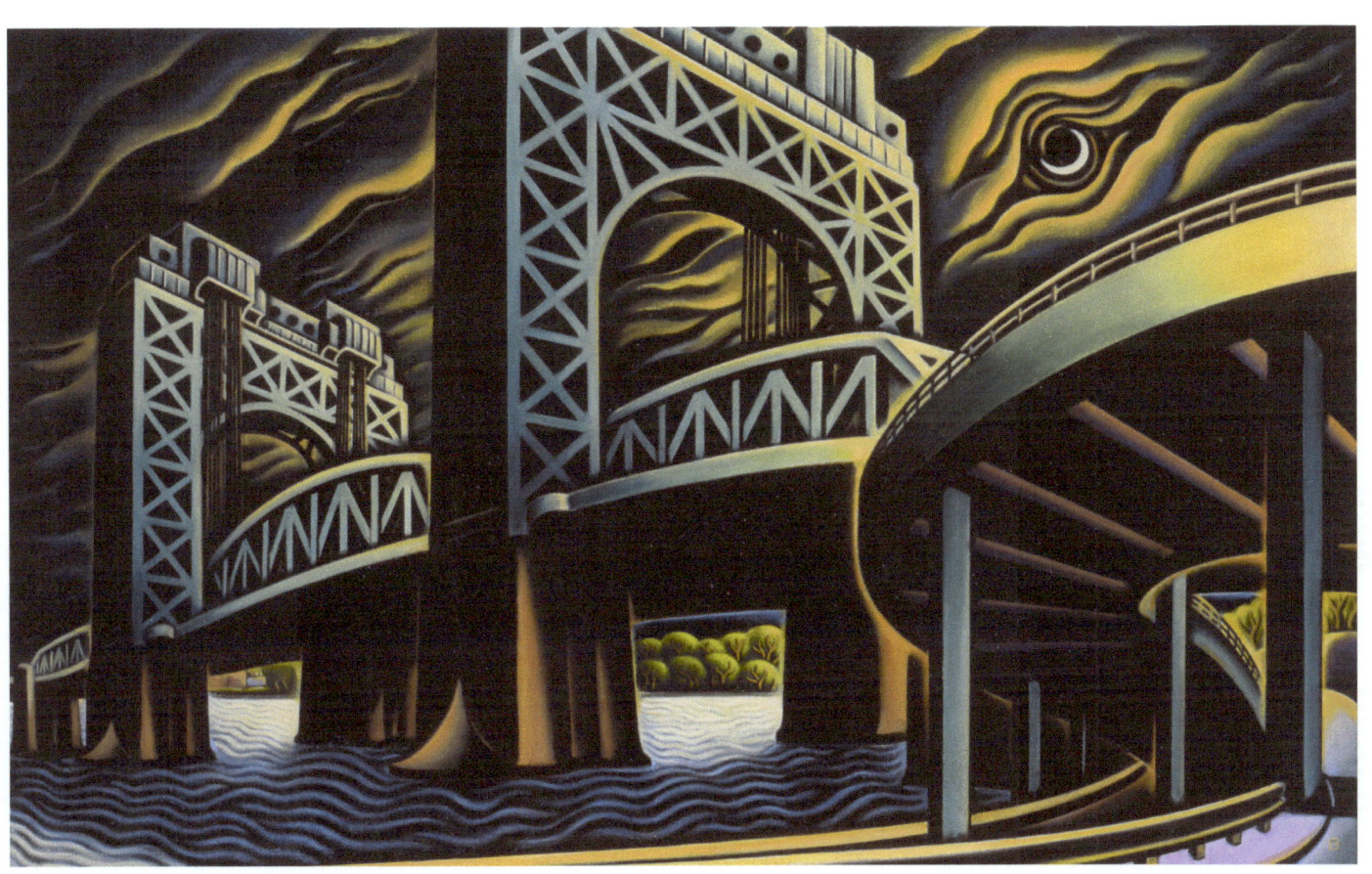

WARDS ISLAND BRIDGE, 2001, oil on canvas, 26" x 52"

Private Collection

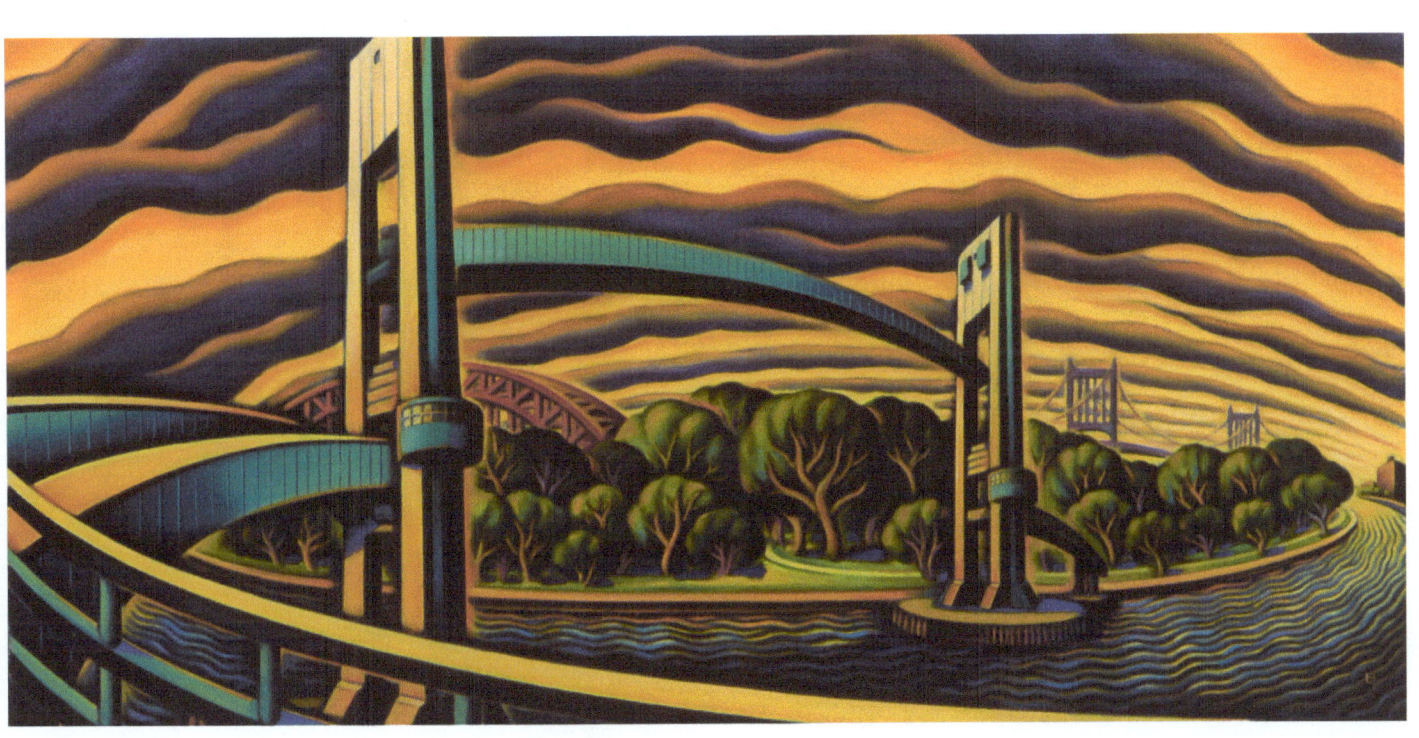

Interview with Bascove by Steven Jay Griffle

SJG It's wonderful to see some of your most famous bridge paintings in person. How did you become interested in bridges?

B In the late 70's I lived in Paris, near the Seine. A fairly active neighborhood, but early Sunday mornings the streets were quiet and blissfully deserted, the perfect time to take my dog on walks along the river. I started taking my watercolors too. Those first bridge watercolors were more like sketches, loose washes in variations of stone colors and pastels. You can't help but think of their history, not only witnesses to untold generations of strolling lovers but hundreds of years of, often turbulent, political change. Moving back to NYC, I again lived near a river, not unusual on this narrow island, and would walk my dog under the Queensboro Bridge. I've painted, photographed, carved, and collaged the Queensboro. It's the one I know best.

SJG I've read that there are more than 2,000 bridges in New York City. Many of them are quite large and famous, most relatively small and modest. What makes you want to paint a particular one? [You seem to know a great deal about each bridge you paint. Do you read about a bridge before you paint it?]

B I've had a wise and powerful muse in the person of the magnificent artist, John Baeder. Privileged to go with him on some of his early scouting for his beloved diners, I saw how he would plan his photographs to catch the light of certain hours of the day, how he loved talking to the owners and employees. He adored everything about diners and roadside eateries. It was his art, his passion, and field of study.

When I first began to paint bridges, they were the ones I saw the most often, the ones that were part of my life. First the Queensboro, and then the three Harlem River Bridges that my husband, architect Michael Avramides, and I would pass on our way to the Bronx, where he's designed and built numerous buildings. My exhibition at the Museum of the City of New York was scheduled at the time of Centennial celebrations of the consolidation of the five boroughs that became New York City. It was the major bridges, crossing over the Hudson and East Rivers, that made it possible. They interconnected the communities, their culture and commerce. Those bridges were essential to include in the show.

Other choices are more serendipitous. The Macombs Dam Bridge was near Michael's favorite mozzarella place, so of course that needed to be explored. A dear friend gave me a ticket to a lecture to hear Margot Ammann Durrer, Othmar Ammann's daughter, speak about her father's engineering marvels. Othmar Amman is considered New York City's master bridge builder, he designed the George Washington, Bayonne, Verrazano-Narrows, Throgs Neck, Bronx-Whitestone and Triborough Bridges. I introduced myself, she knew my paintings of her father's work, we were immediately kindred souls. She introduced me to several members of the audience from the Central Park Conservancy, who asked "Why haven't you painted our bridges?" That began the Central Park project.

Fortunately, I've met several people who are deeply knowledgeable about the romance and history of New York City. The marvelous Barbara Ball Buff, at the Museum of the City of New York, would regale me with some of the City's more eccentric lore. (Did you know that one of the Queensboro's towers housed an artist's studio in the 1920's? It was discovered when the NY Times reported an unusual robbery, a thief had climbed up the tower and stolen several canvases). She also gave me access to the Museum's bountiful Library.

Reading the masthead of the newsletter of the Transit Museum, I found someone else who was besotted with transport. Meeting Laura Rosen, who was, at the time the MTA's Robert Moses Archivist for Bridges and Tunnels, was life changing. Amazingly, it turned out that we had attended the same college a year apart (though brilliant Laura was off to Harvard after graduation). A master photographer, there are two gorgeous books of her work on New York City, THE TOP OF THE CITY, foreword by Brendan Gill, and MANHATTAN SHORES. We are dear friends and my research would be woefully inept without her. She has given fascinating talks at several of my exhibitions. Next spring this wise woman will be bringing her great charm and encyclopedic knowledge to a talk at The Noble Maritime Collection.

SJG Do you usually paint a bridge from real life? Some have very long central spans. How do you decide which perspective to show?

B The bridges are painted from photographs. I try to see each bridge from as many angles as possible, moving all around it, walking across it if there's a foot or bicycle path. Michael will drive me over and back and around it, sometimes the tolls do add up! There will often be several visits, at different times of day and with different light. The paintings are composites of several photographs from various views. The collages are actually a step closer to the original shooting sessions. They are made of dozens of photographs, spliced and joined in spontaneous arrangements. They move and go where they want to go, there is no attempt to show the structure in a readily recognizable form.

SJG You have published three books that combine your passion and talents for painting and reading. What have those experiences been like?

B *STONE & STEEL* originally started as a catalog for my exhibit at the Museum of the City of New York. When my research began I realized that information about dates and construction were of less interest to me than a more deeply felt approach. The words of Gay Talese, Helen Keller, and Lewis Mumford more truly articulated my passion about bridges, and that's what I wanted to share. It must be said that these books were done with David R. Godine, a serious bibliophile, with a well-deserved reputation for beautifully produced books. I had numerous paintings on these subjects and was given full reign to choose the accompanying texts and design the covers. It was a joy.

SJG Looking at your two easels, it seems you are currently focused on creating collage. How does this art compare with your painting?

B Recently I've been mulling over the primal idea that has always driven artists - how to make order out of chaos- and how relevant is that thin boundary between order and chaos? Exploring more abstract forms also means constantly questioning balance and perspective. With enormous pleasure, I've been exploring many of the passions that were only touched on in my previous work - astronomy, engineering, architecture, history, and natural science. Collage has been liberating and great fun for this pursuit. Spirals were always part of the underlying structure of my paintings. Many compositions were based on the Golden Section and the system of Fibonacci numbers. Now I play with images of spiral shells, ammonites and staircases and merge them with overhead views of hurricanes and spiral galaxies. Moons were often in the skies above the bridges in my paintings. I just spent several months making a collage and drawing from a long-loved poem called MOON by Mark Strand. It's probably no surprise that, even in these pieces, books and bridges continue to be essential elements.

SJG   I'm looking forward to seeing your new exhibit at Staten Island's Snug Harbor Cultural Center. What will you be showing? Any new pieces?

 B   The Noble Maritime Collection is one of the jewels of the Snug Harbor Cultural Center. Staten Island is home to New York City's most historical infrastructure. This is a timely exhibition. Several bridges in Staten Island are undergoing major renovations to conform to both modern shipping standards and the growing environmental concerns of the community. The roadbed of the Bayonne Bridge is being raised. Doubtless it will look less elegant, but it's better than destroying the bridge, as first plans suggested. The Goethals Bridge is being completely rebuilt. The replacement will have walking and bike paths and traffic and weather sensors incorporated into its very structure. This November celebrates the 50th Anniversary of the Verrazano-Narrows Bridge, a crucial connection to New York Harbor and to local and regional highway systems.

The new pieces will be of the current Goethals (a requiem) and the Outerbridge Crossing. They are both done in collage and there will be other collage bridges that have never been shown before. Many of the paintings will be on loan from various gracious collectors, so this may be the last time they are together.

Excerpt from an interview in the Summer 2014 issue of StayThirsty.com.

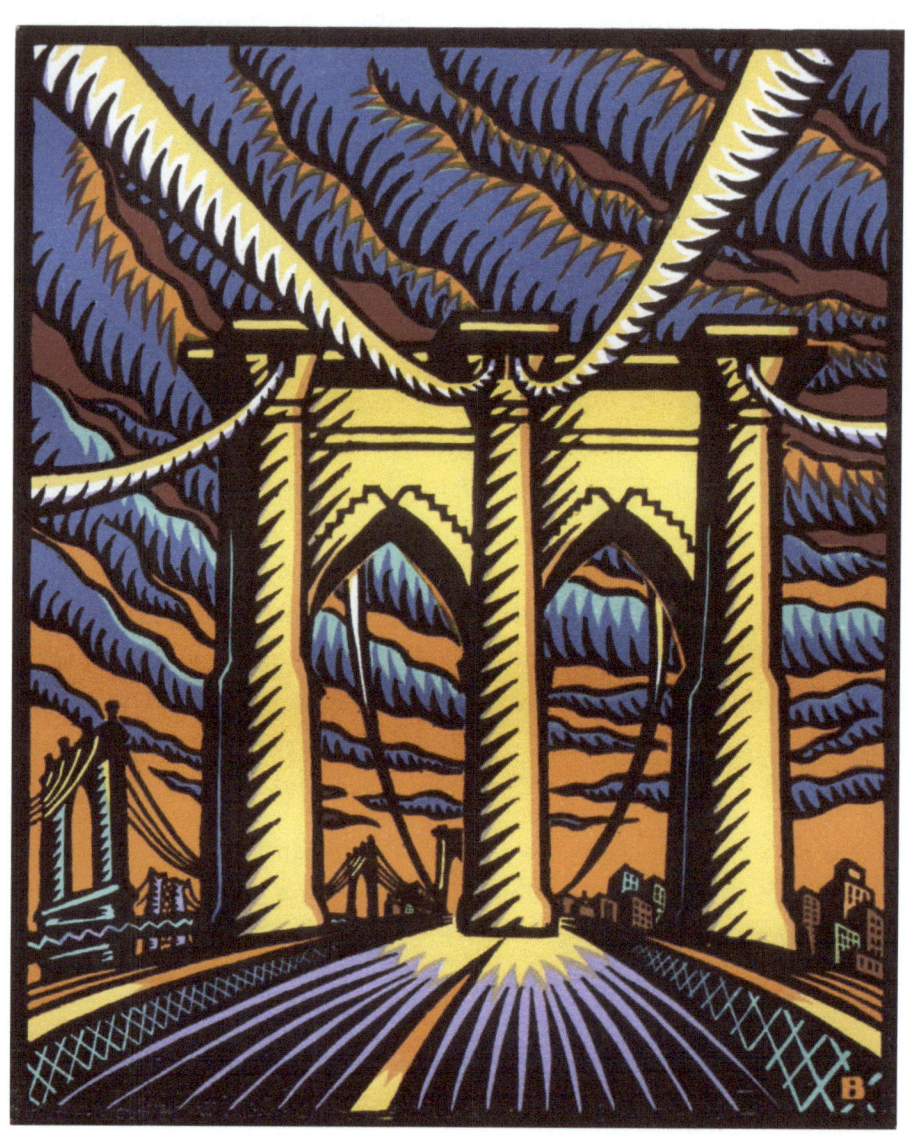

BROOKLYN BRIDGE, 2007, 6 color woodcut & linocut, signed edition of 50, 11 1/8" x 9"

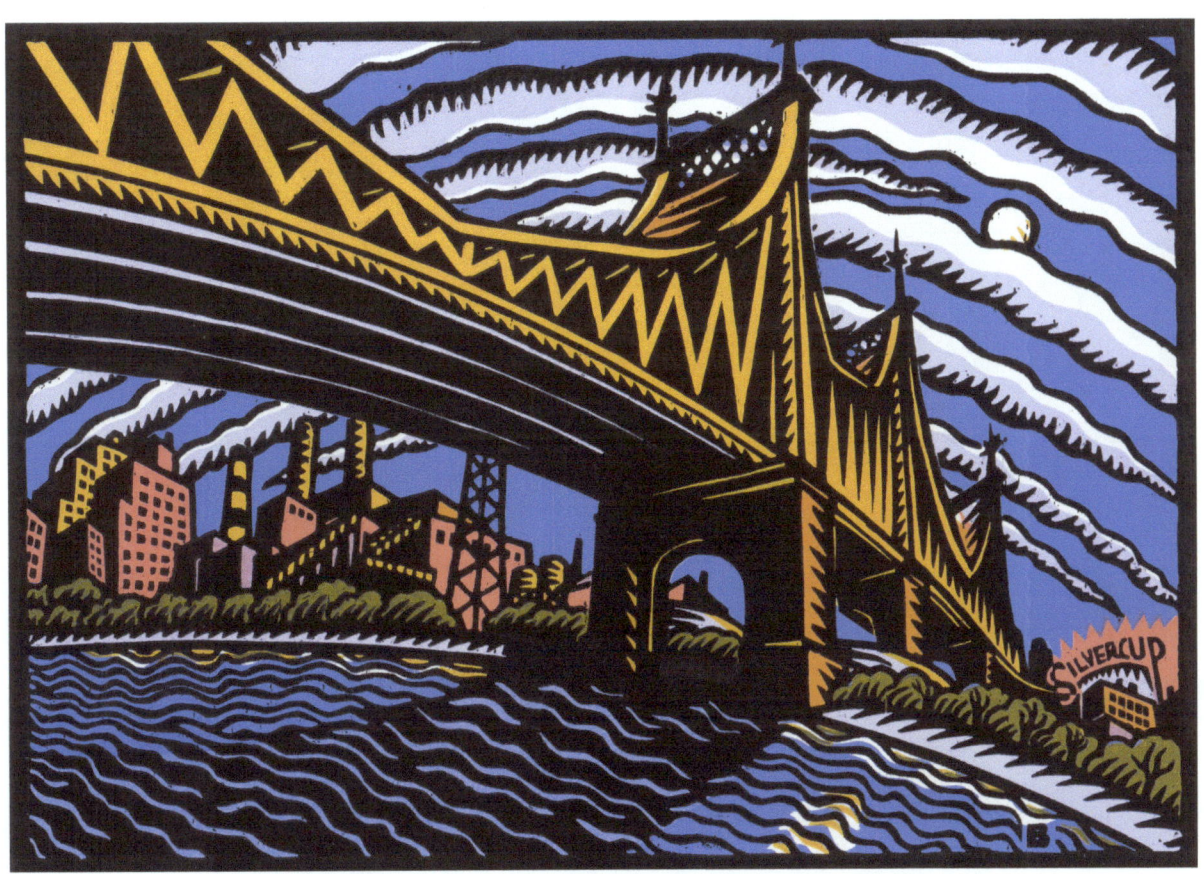

Queensborough Bridge, 2006, 5 color woodcut & linocut, signed edition of 50, 8" x 11"

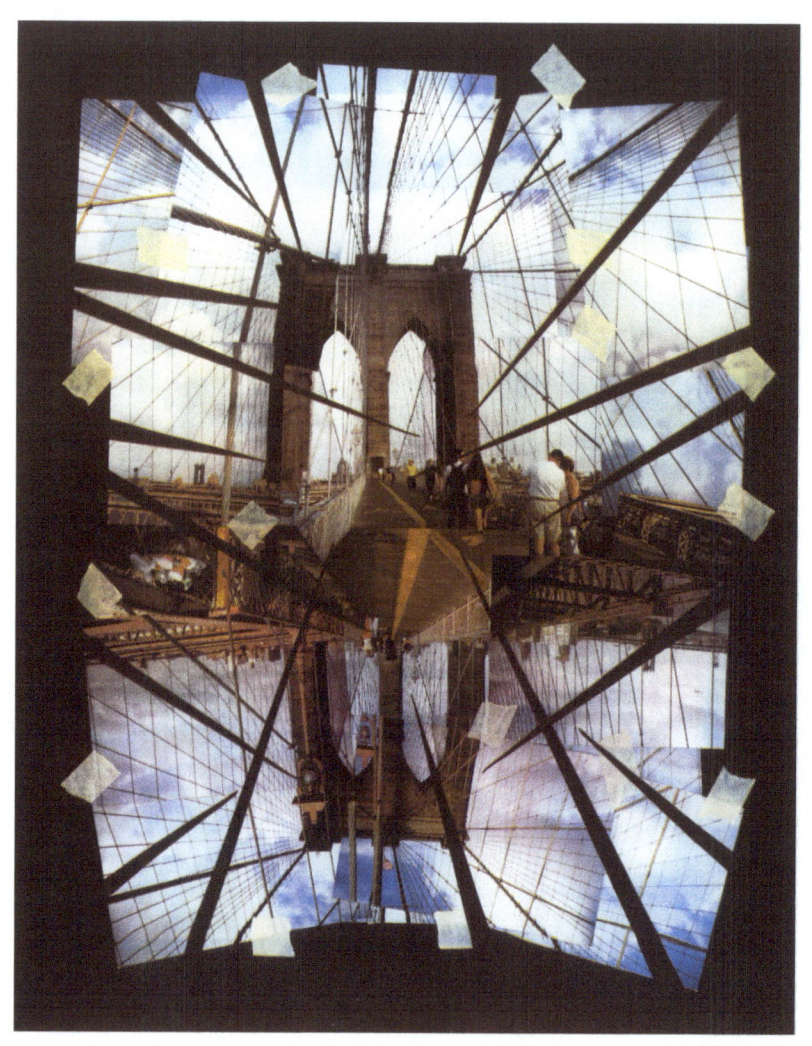

Brooklyn Bridge Erratica I, 2007, silkscreen, signed edition of 30, 23" x 17 7/8"

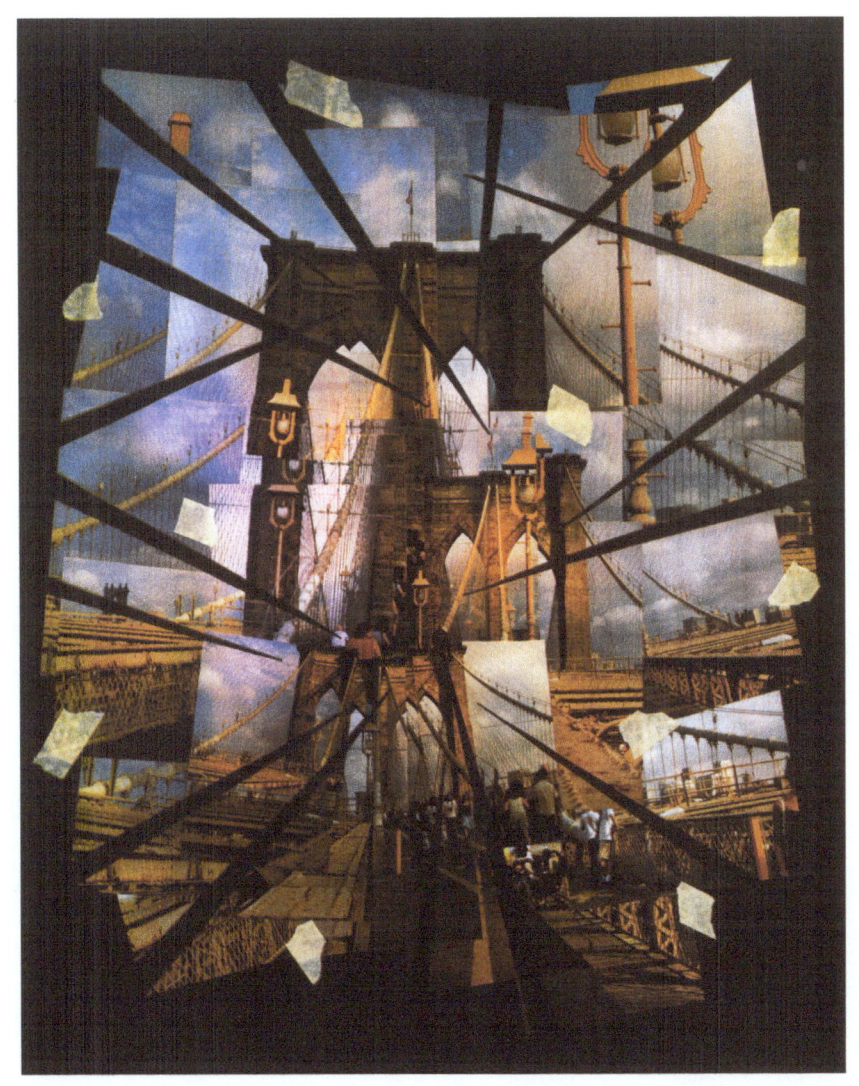

BROOKLYN BRIDGE ERRATICA II, 2007, silkscreen, signed edition of 30, 23" x 17 7/8"

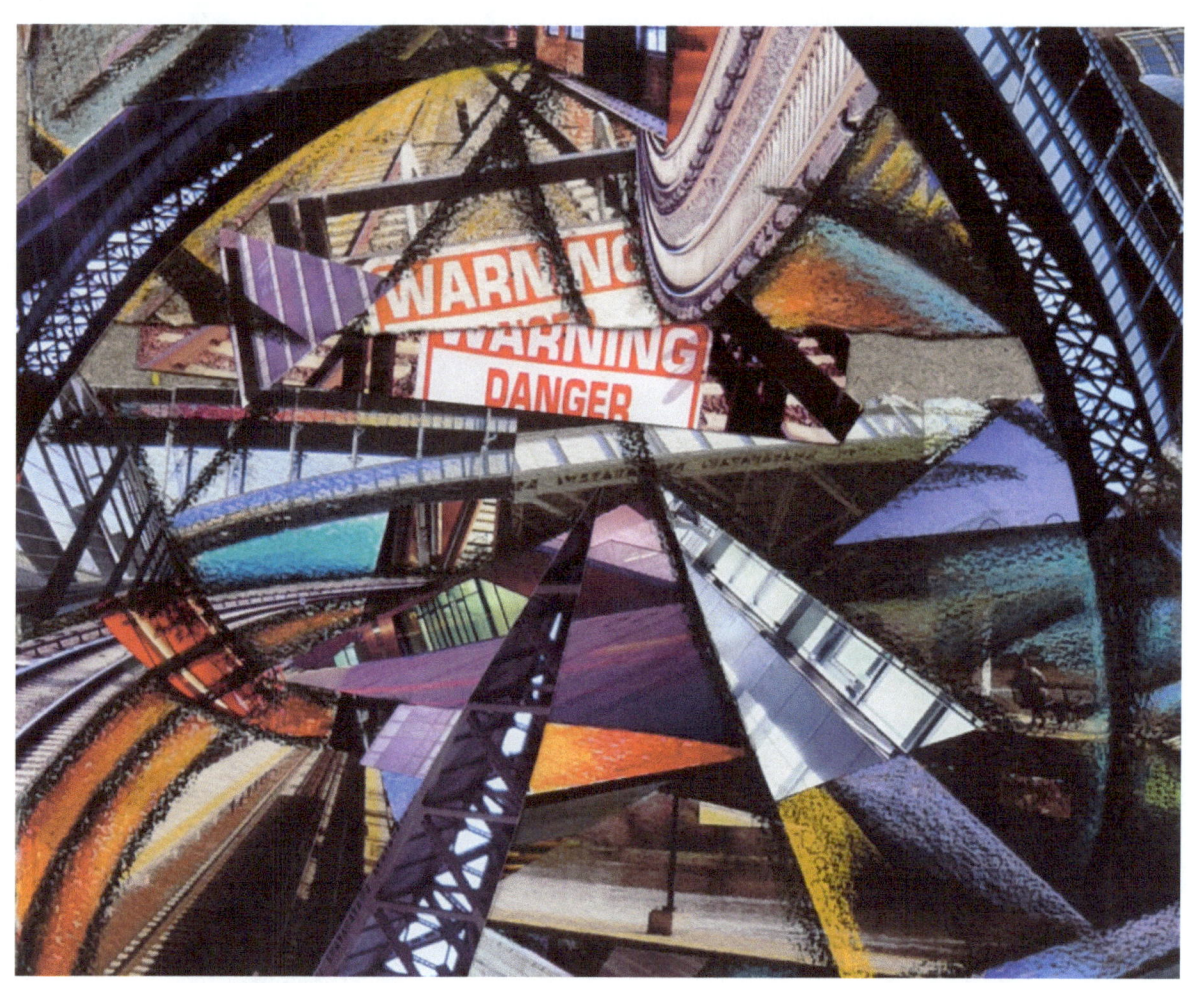

HENRY HUDSON BRIDGE, *detail*

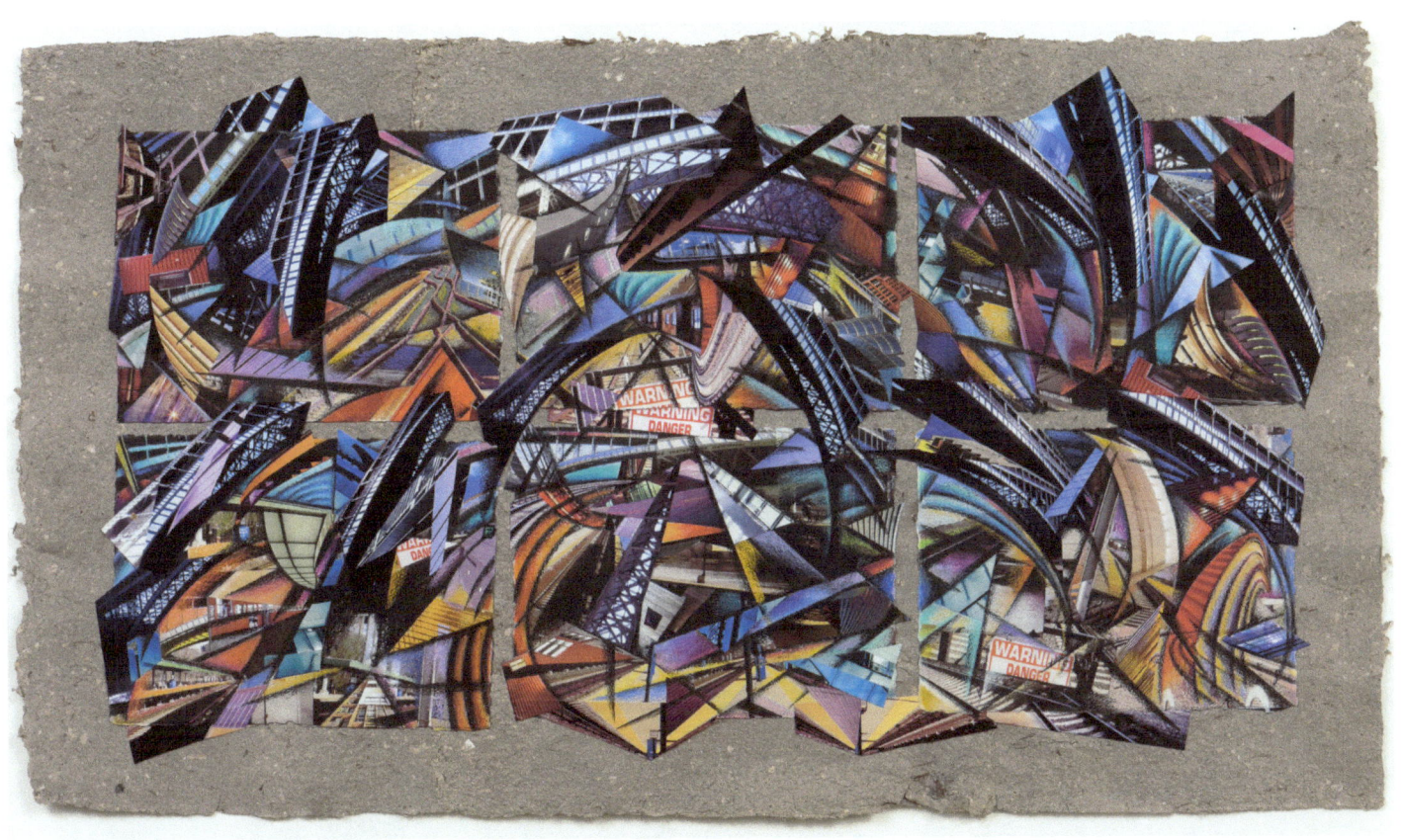

Henry Hudson Bridge, 2012, pigment print, drawing & collage, 23" x 41"

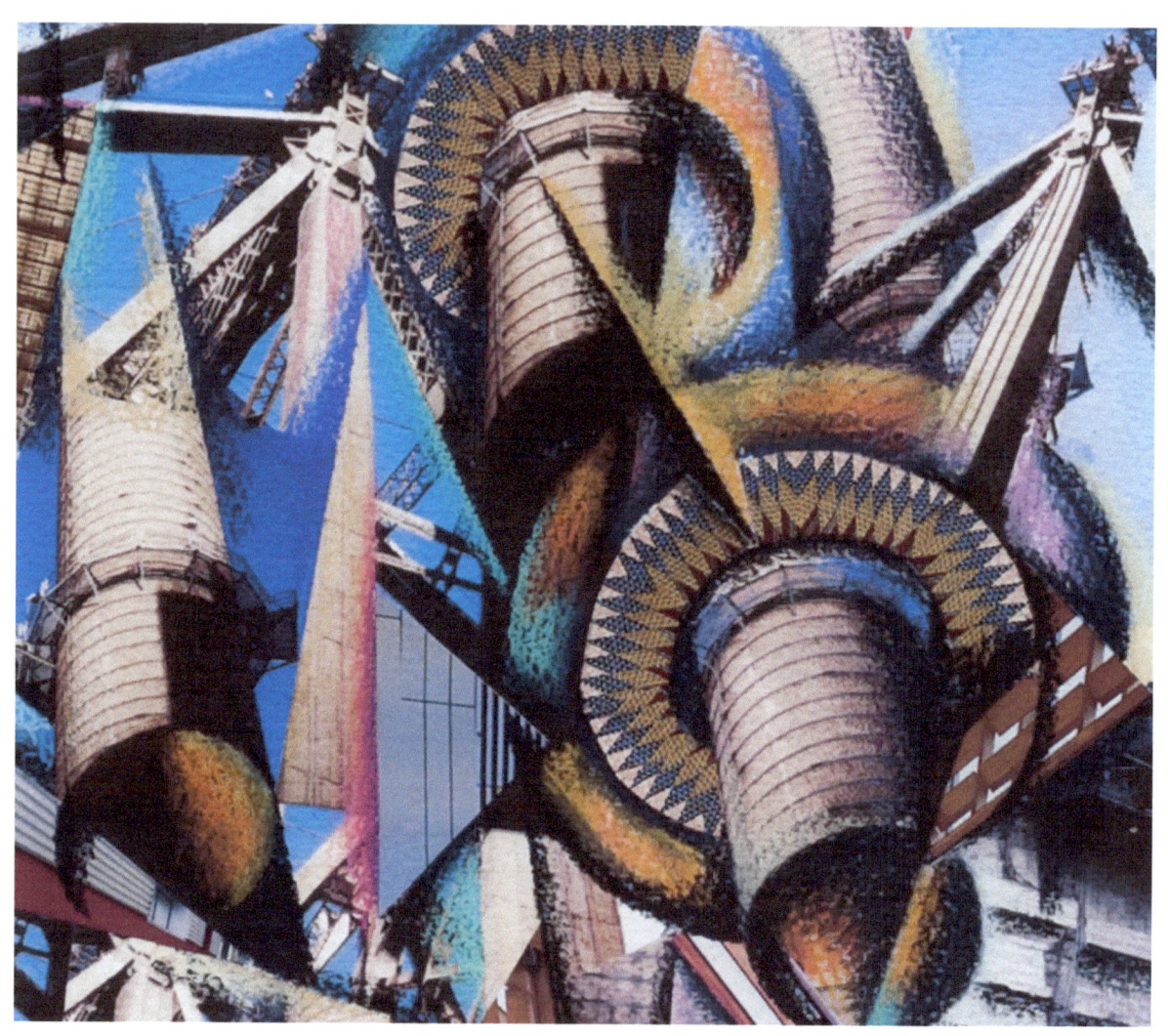

Queensborough Bridge, North – South, detail

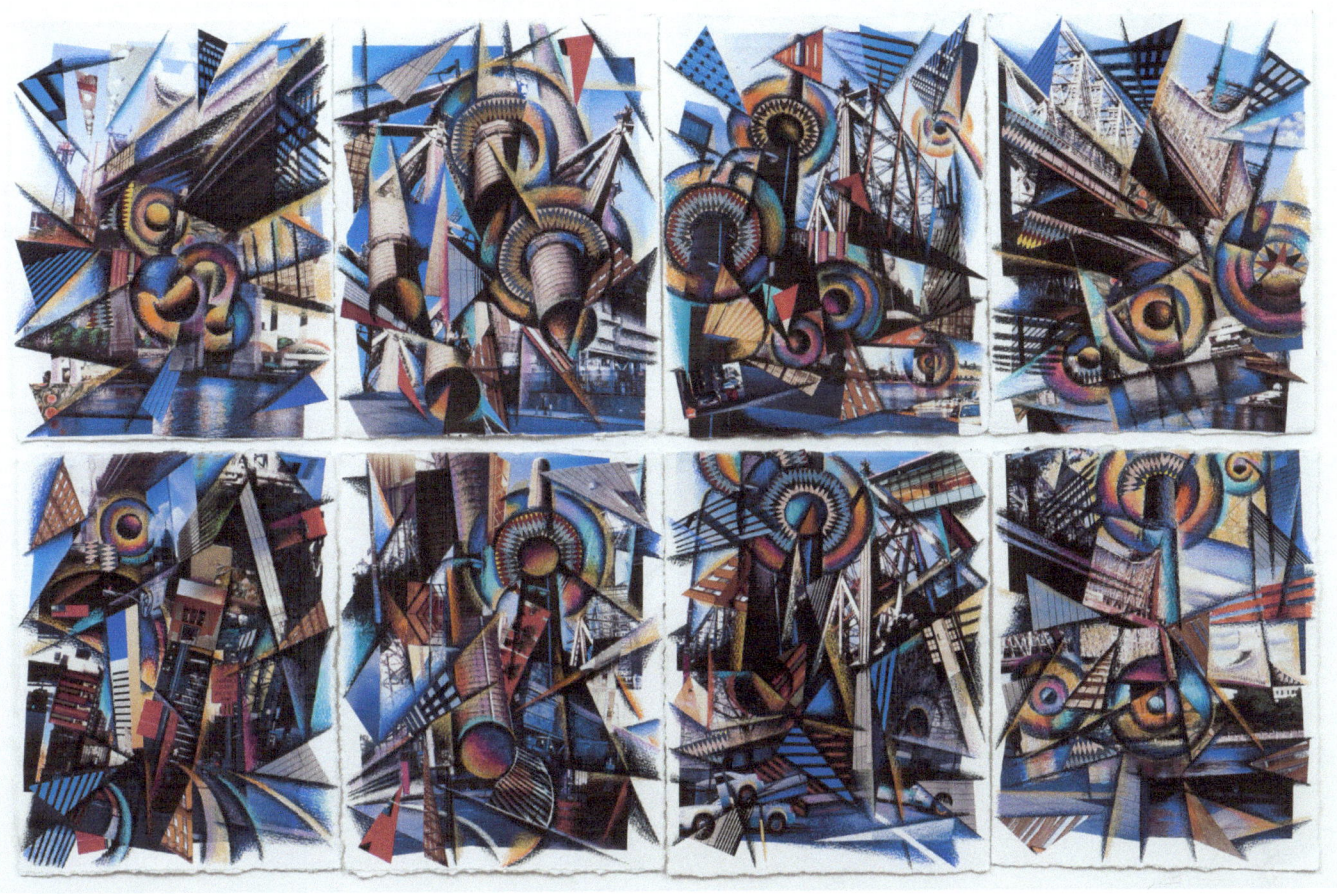

QUEENSBOROUGH BRIDGE, NORTH – SOUTH, 2011, pigment print, drawing & collage, 23" x 34"

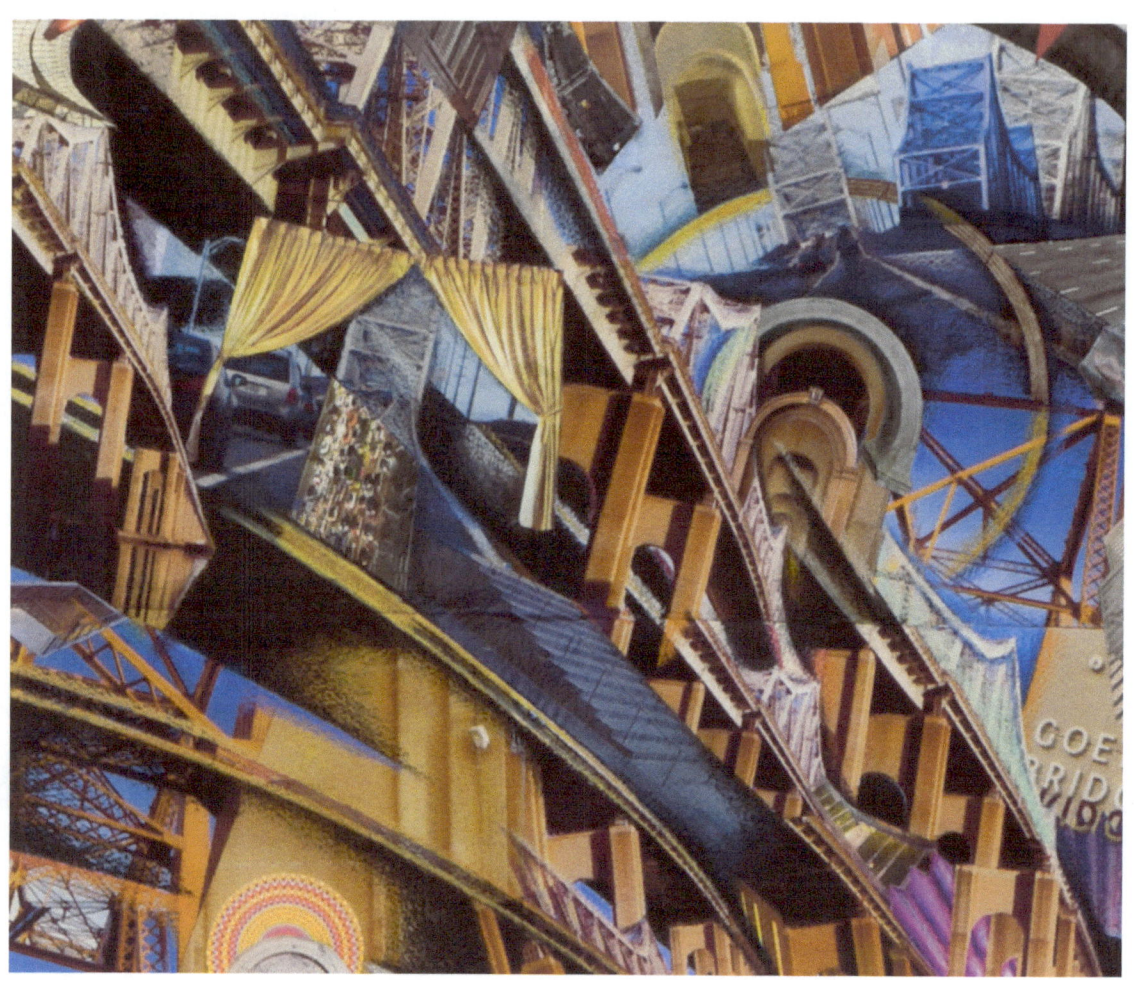

Goethals Bridge (Requiem), *detail*

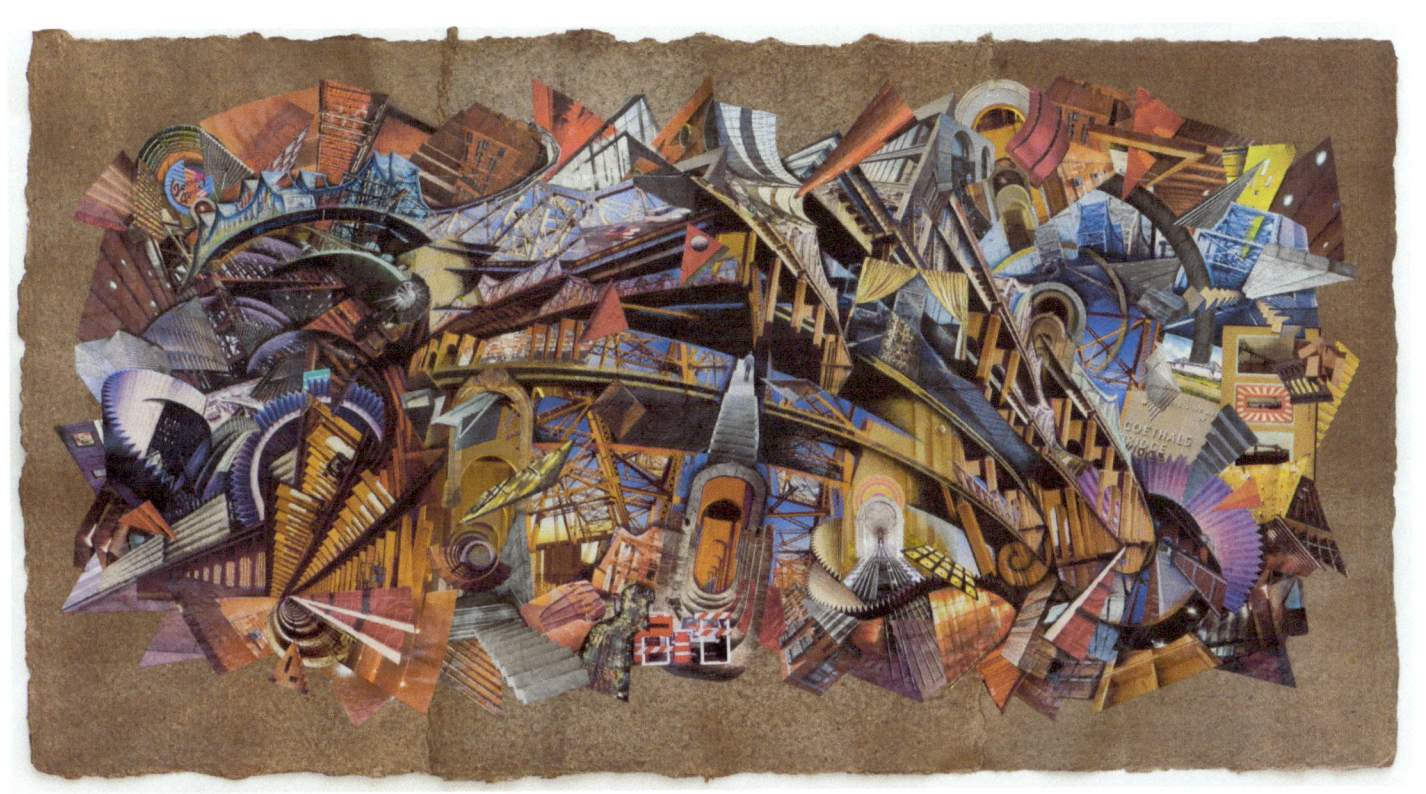

Goethals Bridge (Requiem), 2014, pigment print, drawing & collage, 29" x 54"

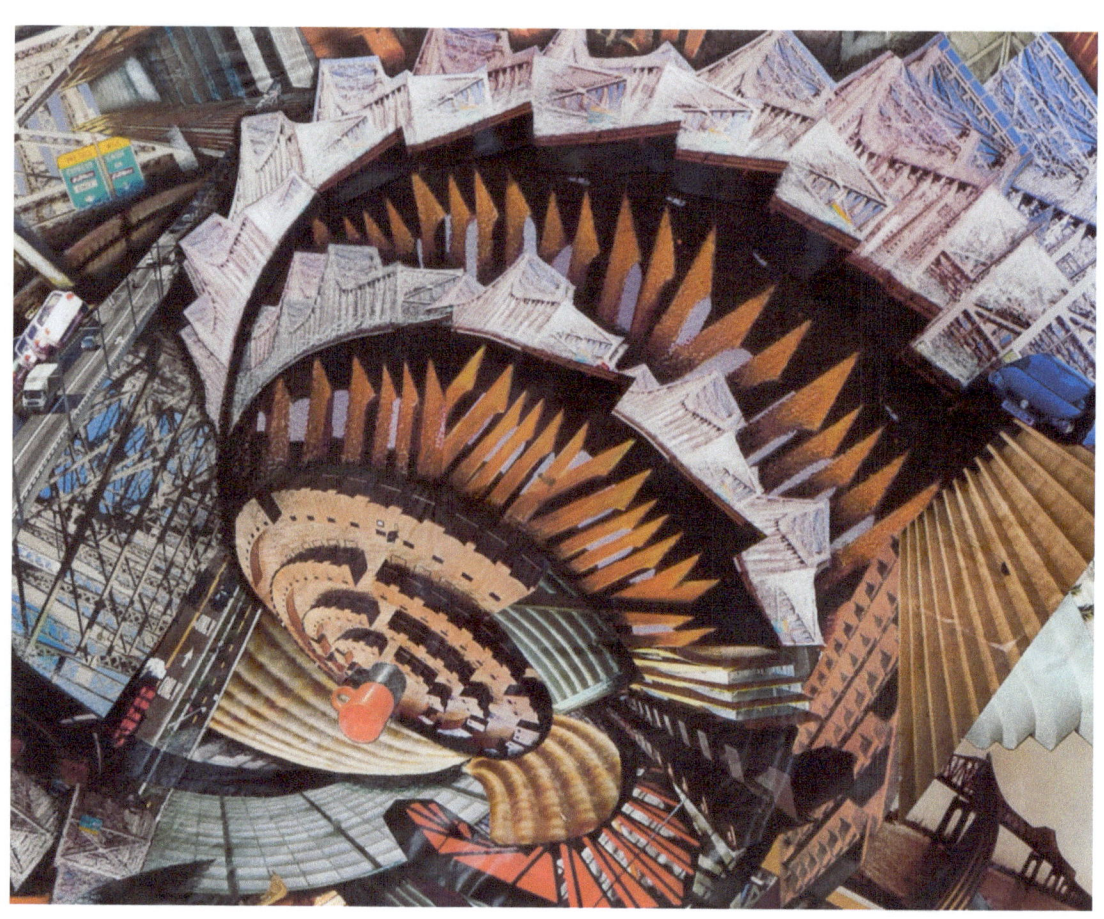

OUTERBRIDGE CROSSING, *detail*

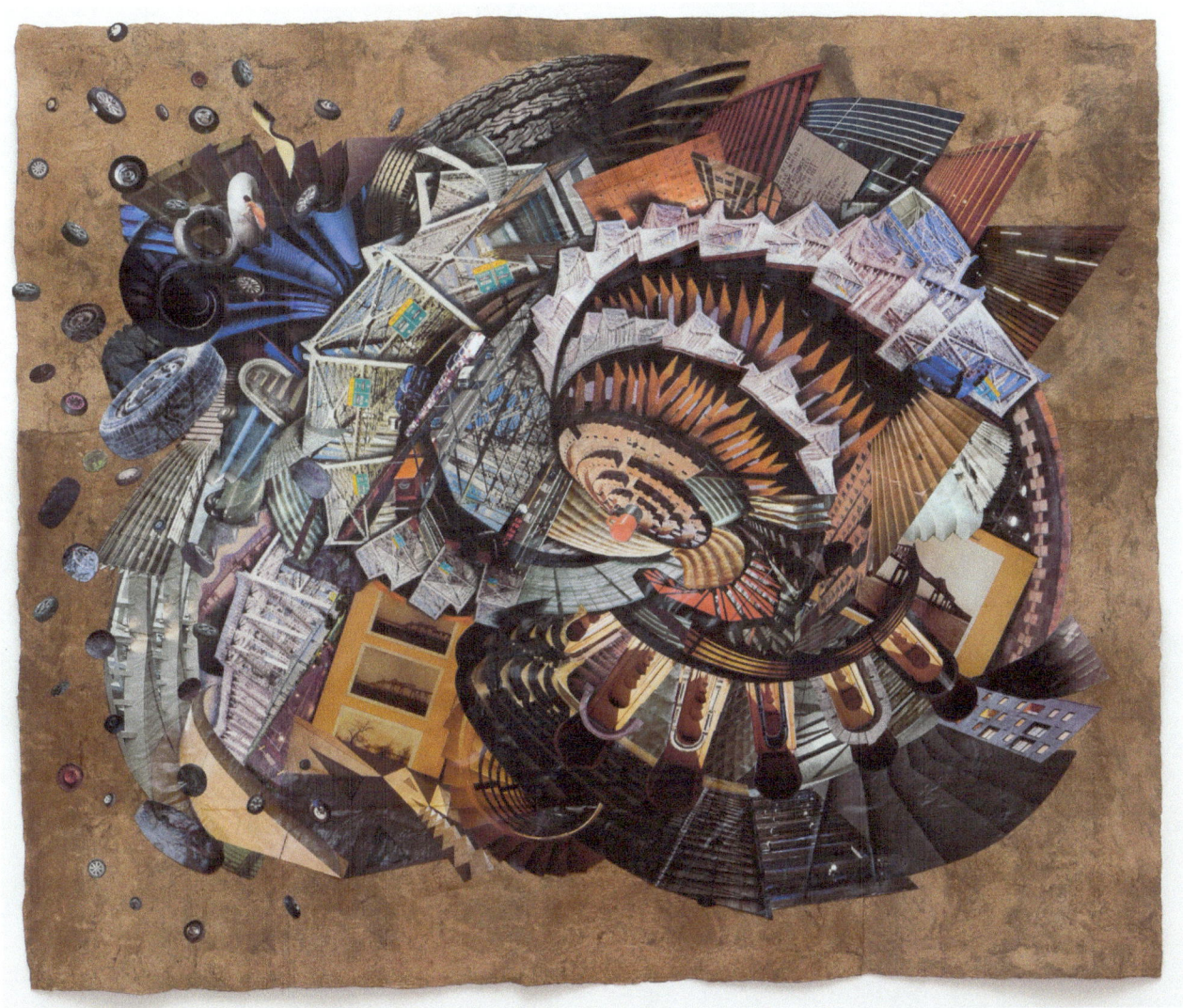

OUTERBRIDGE CROSSING, 2014, pigment print, drawing & collage, 27" x 32"

Public Collections

Museum of the City of New York, Pennsylvania Academy of the Fine Arts, The Linda Lee Alter Collection of Art by Women, Mount Sinai School of Medicine, The Noble Maritime Collection, The Harry Ransom Collection, University of Texas at Austin, The New York Public Library, The Berg Collection, MTA Arts for Transit, The Library and National Archives of Canada, The Wittliff Collections, Texas State University, Musée de Cherbourg.

Solo Exhibitions

2014-15 The Noble Maritime Collection, NY, *Bascove/Bridges Transcending the Metropolis*

2009 The Arsenal Gallery in Central Park, NYC, *Bascove: A Walk In The Park Celebrating the Bridges of Central Park*

2008 Thomas Paul Fine Art, CA, *Bascove: Selected Works*

2007 Uptown Gallery, NYC, *Celebrating the Brooklyn Bridge: Paintings and Works on Paper*

2006 Galerie Luc Queyrel, Paris, *Paris/New York: Ponts/Bridges*

2005 Uptown Gallery, NYC, *Sustenance & Desire: New Works*

Uptown Gallery, NYC, *Dreamwork: New York City Bridges*

The Silo Gallery at The Henderson Cultural Center, CT, *Sustenance & Desire: Still Life, Works on Paper*

2004 Galerie Luc Queyrel, Paris, *Sustenance & Desire: Hommage à Chardin, Scènes de Cuisine*

2003 The Municipal Art Society, NYC, *Monuments of Exaltation: Bascove Celebrates the Bridges of New York City*

Uptown Gallery, NYC, *Monuments of Exaltation: Bascove Celebrates the Bridges of New York City*

2002 Uptown Gallery, NYC, *There Is a Moment: Paintings and Works on Paper*

2001 Galerie Luc Queyrel, Paris, *Where Books Fall Open: Pastels à l'huile*

The Flinn Gallery, CT, *Above and Below: NYC, Bascove and Han Xi*

2000 Uptown Gallery, NYC, *Another Chapter: Books and Bridges*

1999 Galerie Luc Queyrel, Paris, *Women in the City*

1998 The National Arts Club, NYC, *Stone and Steel: Paintings and Drawings of the Bridges of New York City*

The Hudson River Museum, NY, *Stone and Steel: Paintings and Drawings of the Bridges of NYC*

Galerie Luc Queyrel, Paris, *Stone and Steel: Pastels à l'huile*

Museum of the City of New York, NYC, *Stone and Steel: Paintings and Drawings of the Bridges of NYC*

Uptown Gallery, NYC, *New Works: Paintings and Works on Paper*

New York University, Fales Library, NYC, *Stone and Steel: Drawings of the Bridges of New York City*

1997 Jung Institute, Chicago, *The Personal Equation*

1995 Uptown Gallery, NYC, *New Paintings*

1994 University Art Gallery, University of Massachusetts, Dartmouth, *Interior Dialogues*

1993 Uptown Gallery, NYC, *Solace: New Paintings*

1991 Uptown Gallery, NYC, *New Paintings*

Galerie Luc Queyrel, Paris, *Peintures*

1990	Galerie Luc Queyrel, Paris, *Peintures*
1989	Uptown Gallery, NYC, *New Paintings*
	Galerie Luc Queyrel, Paris, *Littérature et Politique*
1987	Barron Arts Center, NJ, *Bascove: Paintings*
	Uptown Gallery, NYC, *New Paintings*
	Galerie Luc Queyrel, Paris, *Bascove: Peintures*
1986	Galerie Luc Queyrel, Paris, *Dentelle: Peintures*

SELECTED GROUP SHOWS

2013	Pennsylvania Academy of Fine Arts, *The Female Gaze: Women Artists Making Their World*
2011	ACA Galleries, NYC, *Summer Group Show*
	The Noble Maritime Collection, Staten Island, NY, *Lifespan: The Bayonne Bridge in Transition*
2010	ACA Galleries, NYC, *Summer Group Show*
2009	Roosevelt Island Historical Society, *Connecting Islands and Generations: The Queensboro Bridge at 100*
	Thomas Paul Fine Art, CA, *24 x24*
2008	Tabla Rasa Gallery, NY, *Bridge as Icon*
	Morrison Gallery, CT, *Group Exhibition*
2007	Gettysburg College, Art Gallery, PA, *The Art of the Gettysburg Review: Representation in Contemporary American Art*
	Thomas Paul Fine Art, CA, *Gallery Artists*
2006	Bachelier Cardonsky Gallery, CT, *Litchfield County Artists*
2005	Memphis College of Art, TN, *Another Voice*
2004	Brooklyn Historical Society, NY, *Beauty Suspended: The Verrazano- Narrows Bridge Turns Forty*
	Maryland Institute College of Art, MD, *Another Voice*
2003	The New York Historical Society, NYC, *Petropolis: A Social History of Urban Animal Companions*
	The Century Club, NYC, *Artists Choose Artists*
2002	Vero Beach Museum of Art, FL, *People Reading: Works from the Collection of Donald Oresman*
	Bachelier Cardonsky Gallery, Kent, CT, *Still Life*
	Elaine Benson Gallery, Bridgehampton, NY, *In the Kitchen*
2001	The Cahoon Museum of American Art, MA, *The Tempting Fruit*
	Bachelier Cardonsky Gallery, CT, *Bascove, Cronin, Runquist*
2000	Museum of the City of New York, NYC, *Painting the Town: Cityscapes from the Museum of the City of New York*
	PaineWebber Art Gallery, NYC, *Painting the Town: Cityscapes from the Museum of the City of New York*
1995	Museum of the City of New York, *Contemporary Cityscape from the Museum of the City of New York*
1994	Parsons School of Design, NYC, *The Women's Room*
1989	Musee de Cherbourg, France, *Vu d'Ailleurs*
1987	Grande Palais, Paris, *Figuration Critique*

Heartfelt thanks to Erin Urban, Ciro Galeno Jr. and the staff at The Noble Maritime Collection, John Baeder, Steven Jay Griffle, Laura Rosen, NYC Department of Cultural Affairs, MTA Arts and Transit, Mary Hedge, MTA Bridges and Tunnels, Krystyna Skalski, Fran Hardy, Nicole Hunter, Joan Peckolick, and Michael Avramides, who makes it all possible.

Pages 38-41 are an excerpt from StayThirsty.com reprinted with permission of Stay Thirsty Media, Inc. Complete interview: http://www.staythirstymedia.com/201407-085/html/201407-griffel-bascove.html